MEMORIES OF
MY WELSH CHILDHOOD

by
John C Thomas

CONTENTS

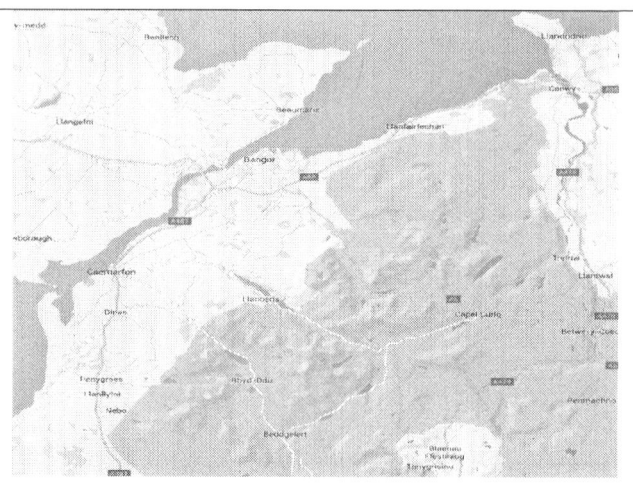

North Wales, Menai Straits

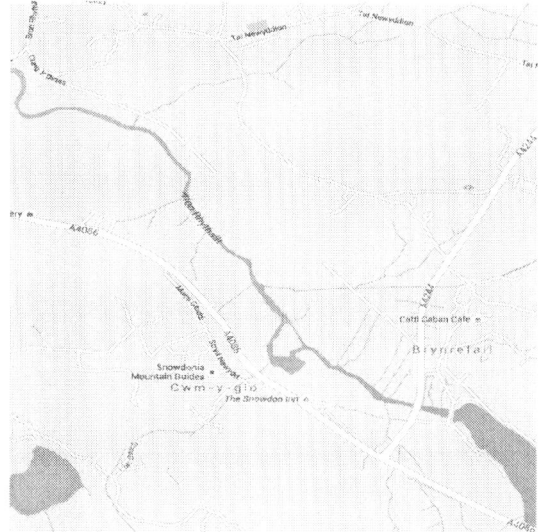

CHAPTER 1

In the beginning
Childhood, the people and the village

I was born on the 28th July 1940 in the small hamlet of Tan-y-Coed near my home village of Cwm-y-Glo; between the two villages were the Llanrug football club ground and Bryn Bras castle.

The place where I was born was a very small cottage: two rooms and a lean-to that served as a kitchen and wash-room, everything else that my mother had to do was done outside by hand: there were no amenities what-so-ever. Now it has had an overhaul and is a modern bungalow, worth a fortune.

The place was primitive, even by the standards of that time and was only to serve as a starter-home until my parents, Mair Eluned Williams and Harry Thomas, found a better place. Our stay there was short and we moved into the village of Cwm-y-Glo to a very small house that was to be our home for many years. All four of my sisters were born in this new home.

I was the oldest child, Betty was next, then Awena, Eluned and Sandra. Mam always said that the German bombers rumbled overhead, negotiating the mountains on their way to bomb the great cities of Liverpool and Manchester while she was in labour. Mam had an older sister, my auntie Mattie. Auntie Mattie was the only close relation she had and her help was vital as my mother struggled to find her feet as a young woman. I was to get very close to my aunt and spent a lot of time with her before and after she married uncle Bob. Our friendship lasted a lifetime, and as and when each of my sisters came along I would be sent to Pwllheli to stay with her.

5

Mam and Auntie Mattie had a very difficult upbringing and when my mam and dad met my mother was in service in Llanrug. Mother was nineteen and father was a confirmed bachelor in his thirties.

Their life together was full of ups and downs, but the early years for us children were nothing but joy and happiness and the complete freedom that our area provided for us.

Dad had family all over the area. The three branches of the family: the Thomas's, the Roberts' and the Jones's all lived closely around. My paternal grandmother, Elizabeth Roberts, was the oldest person in the village. She had married first to Lewis Azaraiah Thomas, her next door neighbour in New Street which was her childhood home. He was a lot older than her and possibly in those days in a small village finding a partner was not easy. She was just seventeen when they married and after his death she re-married to John Roberts, a bachelor who had lived and worked at a near by farm for many years. He only returned to live in the village when he married my grandmother. John Roberts was revered and loved by his step children and by the whole community, he was a deacon in the chapel. He also came from one of the oldest village families (the Roberts family of Bryn Ffynnon).

Bryn Gro, where my family lived, was the middle house in a terrace of three. The owner would turn up every Friday night for his rent that had to be paid in cash. The house was lit by a combination of electric lights and paraffin lamps; heat came from a coal fire; a boiler and a mangle in the back yard provided laundry facilities; the toilet was at the top of the garden in a small hut with the normal News-of-World toilet paper; Army great coats were the blankets for the beds. All the water for domestic use had to be carried for some way, up a steep hill each and every morning, all of us children would help out with this task.

My friend Richard Jones and myself would also take water to Kate Thomas, one of the neighbours, as she had a bad leg and her son, also John Thomas, had started work, being a bit older than us.

There were several boys called John Thomas in our village, so to differentiate between us we were called by our mother's or father's Christian name, or the house that we lived in. I was known as John Bach Ty Capel. The son of Kate Thomas was known as John Kate Thomas.

My life long friend was Richard Jones; we lived next door at Bryn Gro and went to school together and when we both left the village we seemed to get closer.

Another man who I shared my name with was the aforementioned John (Kate) Thomas. He was to become a great friend in the last few years of his life. We had not been school friends and had not been close as youngsters; John was slightly older and would have his own pals. He was very popular with the village community because of his boyhood job of delivering bread for the village baker.

I had not forgotten John or his mother Kate Thomas or even his grandfather Tom Thomas, as my own mother had insisted after John Kate had started work, that we filled his mother's water buckets each morning from the communal tap that was some distant from her home. It was a task that Richard and I did every morning before school, Kate was disabled and would not have been able to do it herself. In the village we helped one another.

Richard's mother was the rock my own mother needed to bring up her own family in dire circumstances. Mrs Jones had her own problems, but each one of my sisters never forgot her and would visit whenever they came to Wales.

Mrs Jones, who lived next door, was a wonderful lady who was the friend, tutor and everything else to my overworked mother. My own mother had had a falling out with her mother, my maternal grandmother, and there was no contact between them. I only met my maternal grandmother Mary Williams once, and that was very briefly. Mrs Jones' youngest son, Richard, was to become my life long friend. A friendship that I have treasured and have always regarded him as a brother.

When I was a child: Richard's father was then alive, as were his three brothers Tom, John Morris and Geraint. There was never a time when any of my sisters and myself did not visit Mrs Jones when we came back to Wales to visit or on holiday, after we had moved to Corby.

My grandmother was known as Lizzie, or Nain Cwm (to the younger family members). She was the matriarch of the family and commanded the respect of everybody, but in my childhood she was old and infirm. And I loved her to bits.

My home village of Cwm-Y-Glo in my childhood days was a wonderful place for a child. Street lighting was a thing of the future, but we had shops, school, two chapels and the church, and a village hall.

Watkins was the baker and the bakery was very popular with children and grown ups. There was a shop called Shop Eric, and further along Llew Hughes had the main shop in the village. I remember so well getting half a banana outside his shop. I had never seen a banana let alone tasted one, it was the first supplies of bananas he had received after the war. I bit into the fruit, skin and all. Megan had the station shop near to the Railway hotel

8

(fricsan). There were one or two other shops as well.

Many years later, Richard Jones, John (Kate) Thomas and myself went to visit Llew Hughes at the nursing home in Penisarwaen. He was very old by this time, but alert and without any prompting knew us and related stories regarding our respective families. The three of us treasured that visit.

Tan-y-Graig, or Ty Capel, as it was in my time, was to be my home during my growing up years.   This was my grandmother's home. At first my eldest sister, Betty, had lived with Nain Cwm, but as my sisters grew older it was felt by my parents that I should not be sharing a room with them so Betty came home and I went to live with Nain. It was very close to home so I could see my family every day, whenever I wanted.

I went to the village primary school and then to Bryn Eryr, the church school, and finally left the village at 14 years old to attend H.M.S. Conway naval college in Anglesey.

I remember very well my teacher at the village school. She had a limp or may have lost her leg, it was said that she lost her leg in an accident involving a train? I never found out the truth.

At Bryn Eryr, Williams was our teacher; he was from Llanberis and had been in the Royal Navy. All the boys in our class thought the world of him, but he was not to be crossed and ran a tight ship. Richard and I would often see him in the pub, many years after we had left school.

Having left H.M.S. Conway to join Port Line Ltd, I enjoyed a short period at sea. During this time my family had moved to Corby in Northamptonshire to find work and when I came home having left the merchant navy, I found Corby a town that had plenty of work in the steel works, and Dad arranged for me to continue my apprenticeship with Stewart and Lloyds (S&L) at the Tube Works.

Dad moved to Corby in the early 1950's after he found himself with no work in Wales. The Dinorwig Slate Quarry was coming to the end of its slate producing life and when the chance to move came about he was not keen to move, but Mam was and with five children that in due course would need employment, there was very little option in her view.

The irony of the situation was that by this time my parents had become eligible for a new house and had just moved to Brynyrefail, a village the other side of the river Seiont, some three miles away using the bridge at Pen-y-Bont. A house called Trem Eilian was to be our home for a year or two, I was to commute between the two villages as Ty Capel was my main abode. Nain Cwm was needing care and caring was completely different in those days to how it is today and had to be undertaken in the best way possible within the family.

My grand mother had never crossed the border to England. The furthest she had ever been was to Porthmadog to visit her sister.

My parents at long last had been allocated a new council house in the next village of Brynyrefail, but I continued to attend the school at Cwm-y-Glo as I was at my grandmother's home, Ty Capel, most of the time.

My grandmother's best friends were Catherine Jane Green, Mrs Green next door who was related somehow to Catherine, Mrs Hughes Gromlech (Maldwyn's mother), Mary Ann, of Mona House. Many others would call at regular intervals, men and women. Frank D.M. was a colourful character who had a taxi and car-hire business and he would always call round. Frank chewed his tobacco like an old cow chewing cud and also moved his false teeth round and round in his mouth; I was fascinated.

Another character was the Wallpaper Lady. She would appear now and again to wallpaper and clean the back room. Coal fires and paraffin lamps make an awful greasy black mess. In those days the rolls of paper had to be edged – trimmed with a pair of scissors. She had mastered it to a fine art and each move of the scissors was matched by opening and closing her mouth. Again I was fascinated.

Another odd pair were Dan and Hannah. Dan was a cobbler from the old school and he worked from an old cottage in Brynyrefail but lived with his sisters at a house in Rhallt Goch in the village. This was a place where I spent a lot of time, whenever it rained I would play with my friend Gwyn Rawlands there, mostly indoors, as Gwyn had a bad chest. Dan had lost an eye as a youngster, but was a first class tradesman. He had found good business in mending and re-modelling the heavy boots the quarrymen used. Whenever the boots had been worn beyond repair Dan would use the upper and convert it to a clog, you could have rubber or metal soles. His sister Hannah wore Wellington boots summer and winter.

Harry and his brother Llew would also visit Ty Capel now and again to deliver a load of logs for the fire and a colourful pair they were. Harry lived for a time in Craig-y-Don.

My friends was plentiful , Gareth Philips (Phips), Gareth Roberts, Cecil Morris, Gwyn Rowlands (Rallt Goch), Eurwyn Williams (Llwyncoed) and many others.

Life in the village was not all work. We had plenty to do

11

especially in the summer. Winter was long with very little to occupy us youngsters, but the summer was completely different. Traffic going through the village was increased by the summer visitors to the area, cyclists were common in large groups going through the village (no bypass in those days), tour buses (charabancs as we called them) from Llandudno and the other coastal resorts frequently came through.

One of our adventures and pastimes was swimming in the river under supervision of some of the older children. Another was sliding down the two slides behind Cwt Hers (the shed that an old hearse was kept in). Directly behind the shed was the polished rock that we used as a slide. We graduated from slide bach (short slide) to slide fawr (long slide) and the steepest. They both offered a challenge and many times I had a wet bum by miss-timing my slide and finishing in the pool of water that always seemed to be at the very bottom. Clothing was another problem with sliding; the girls would tuck their skirts into their knickers; the boys would have to be very careful not to wear out their trouser bottoms.

Further up the hill was "Hendre Jiggott" and Pen Bwich the most wonderful place on earth. It held some sort of magic that even us children felt but could not understand.

Playing football with my great pal Cecil Morris in a small green space at the top of the hill next to Rhallt Goch was a thrilling two-a-side kick about – one of us would kick - first to 10 goals, then change over goal-keeper to kicker, we would spend hours at it. If we had more than two players we would sometime go to the old tennis courts and if it was a proper game the school playground or Cae Bach could be used. The best player was Melvin Prichard, he could hold his own with the men.

The village hall was out of bounds for us youngsters and was used mainly by the men for billiards and snooker, my dad included.

We never had a need for a clock or a watch as the blasting at the quarry gave us the time. Heavy lorries ran through the village continually carrying bombs and ammunition that had been stored at Chwarel Glyn during the war, they dumped their loads at sea, so the rumours went.

I mentioned "Cwt Hers" earlier. This was a shed that housed the horse drawn hearse, not in use when I was a boy, but it was still there under lock and key. We could see it through the window but were never allowed in. Who held the key, heaven knows!

Football played a big part in my life as a boy. Llanrug played near Bryn Bras Castle and they had a very good team. My mother's cousin by the name of Dick Williams known as Dick Plas from Rhosgadfan, played in goal. He would always appear in a green polo neck jumper and a cap.

There were several annual events held in the area.

The fireworks night organised by Watkins was a special night. He would gather combustible material for weeks and store it in an old building, building the frame for weeks beforehand. How he saved the money to buy the fireworks, I do not know.

A carnival was held every year, Cwm-y-Glo had the prettiest girls in the area so it was said and I am sure that is true. The Sunday School trip was a big highlight: Sunday school, the Band–of-Hope and St John's Ambulance could be attended each week and as there was nothing else to do they were well attended.

Travelling out of the village was becoming normal as people had started working in other employment rather than in the quarries like our fathers. Young people converged on our home town of Caernarfon on a Saturday as did others from all the surrounding areas. Caernarfon would be teeming with young people on Saturday evening, the last two buses out of town would be packed solid with everyone making their way home.

My childhood in the village was a joy, I had freedom, our own language and wonderful people who cared about me, what more could a child want?

Cwm-y-Glo prior to the by-pass being built and when the railway ran through the village. In the background is the bridge that all the village children played on; to the right of the bridge was Cae Bach, our only playing field. To the left Capal Mawe can be seen and just below Shop Fawr that was demolished in the 1950s.

The entrance to the goods yard, taken from the main line looking towards the village. The Railway Hotel can be seen in the background.

View of the station and goods shed taken from the rocks overlooking the station.

Cwm-y-Glo station was opened to traffic on 1st July 1869 and served the area, partly in a cutting. Access was made through a rocky outcrop which was also bridged by the Cae -marfon to Llanberis road. As there was more passenger traffic a public house was built called Fricsan or the Railway Hotel. A small shop was also built at the entrance near the gate, called Megan's Shop.

After the Second World War the excursion traffic declined. The site and whole track system was removed and incorporated into the main road, the village being bypassed.

A front view of the station and platform with the road bridge, looking towards the village through the railway arch.

Richard Jones, (Bryn Gro); John Thomas (Ty Capel); Cecil Morris (Rallt Goch)

Richard Jones; John Evans; John Thomas and John (Kate) Thomas

CHAPTER 2

Llwyncoed Farm

Whenever I went to my mother's house after school I would accompany my class mate, Eurwyn Williams, along the main road towards Llanberis as he lived at his parents' farm, Llwyncoed. We would argue and bicker most of the way but when we reached the little field that housed Bell, the shire horse, the arguing stopped. Bell was the last horse to have worked on the farm and Mr Williams had retired her to this small field near to the bridge at Pen-y-Bont; a shelter had been provided for her at one corner. We would gather fresh grass from the roadside to give her. We all loved Bell, she was good tempered and loved the attention, we would never hurt her in any way.

Llwyncoed farm was my favourite place and like many of my class mates, I would head for the farm to join Eurwyn in some great adventures, also Mrs Williams was a close friend of my father having been at school with him. Many years later, I remember driving my dad from Corby so he could see some relations of Mrs Williams, visiting from South Africa.

Mrs Williams was a lovely lady. She would give us a glass of butter milk and a bit of cake before sending us on our way home, and sometimes an apple or two from the orchard in the summer. I also remember very well the living room because of the guns that hung on the wall, we would have loved to have a go at them, but they were not to be touched.

Eurwyn was the youngest of the four Williams brothers, I remember Noel but not the others.

The farm buildings I remember very well: the cowshed,

the pig sties, a barn that was used for boiling up the swill for feeding the pigs. In the loft above we would be warm and cosy in the winter playing Monopoly. Through the cow shed into another barn, there was a circular saw that was used for cutting fence-posts and logs for the fire place. Through the back door and there was a stream that ran behind the buildings. The farm in those days employed a farm hand - a wonderful little man who lived in the village called John Philips.

Through the back door and over the stream, and you would find yourself in the woodland and further on you would come on to a small patch of green with a tree in the middle and a wall round it creating a small field. Mr Williams would keep half a dozen tubs (rams) with their front leg and back leg tied together to keep them away from the ewes. The clearing was also the home of the farm bull and we youngsters held him in awe.

This leads me to a story of one day when a small group of us were the Red Indian Braves under the leadership of "Phips" Gareth Philips and decided to visit the field. We had done it before and never had any reaction from the bull so we very quickly got fed up with the adventure. This time however was slightly different. After throwing a few twigs at the gentle beast he decided to walk toward us. This triggered a mad dash by the not-so-brave Indian troops heading for the tree. Leading from the front, was Gareth Roberts who for better or worse, had climbed on to a long branch. Phips scampered up, stalling half way so that the last pair had no room to get up the tree trunk. They turned to head for the wall at speed.

The branch was very strong on which Gareth Roberts found himself and held his weight with ease but the further he went the more it sagged downwards and with the rest of the troops dancing up and down at the trunk end, the more it sagged. Anyway the old bull ambled towards the tree directly under the sagging branch then stopped wondering what the commotion was. I dare say he then decided to nudge the branch with his nose (the ring and all). This was to cause panic. Gareth Roberts screaming in fear, the brave Indians shouting with joy.

After a while the noise was heard down at the farm and the farm-hand appeared. The troops dashed for the cover of the wall leaving Gareth to fend for himself. The farm-hand walked up to the bull, scratched behind his ear and led him away. The troops finally retreated back to the village very pleased with themselves, all except one!

Another animal that was a subject of our attention was a billy goat that had been housed behind a fence to stop us entering a clearing that led to very deep ponds (pull heli). They were situated between Craig-y-Don and Cwt Hers just under the road bridge. This animal took no prisoners and would charge head down, however it did not stop us tormenting him but only from safely behind the fence. I have no idea who owned him.

Cwym-y-Glo primary school

Two John Thomas's look round Bryn Eryr School
and Cwm-y-Glo primary school

CHAPTER 3

Trem Eilian Brynyrefail.

After being on the waiting list for a council house for many years my parents were suddenly allocated a new house in the village of Brynyrefail some three miles from Cwm-y-Glo, using the bridge at Pen-y-Bont, but only a short distance as the crow flies. The only problem was having to cross the river Seiont and some very boggy ground, a trip I was to undertake many times as a boy. It was very unsafe if the river was in flood or winter time when the water could be frozen.

This event of moving was to cause a lot of unrest in the family, my mother was very unhappy about me being at Ty Capel, and having a new house and the bedroom space, she wanted me home.

Also my uncle Owen (Now Bach) and family had been allocated the next door house to us, although his family did not stay long at Trem Eilian owing to the same set of circumstances as we were facing at Ty Capel: caring for auntie Lizzie's ageing parents at Bryn Gwynedd in the village of Carmel some miles away. They decided to move to the family home of Bryn Gwynedd: the house is still in the family to this day.

This was not an easy decision to make for them, with a family: my cousins Edwin and Mary to consider, and uncle Owen's work in another area meant he had to live during the week at Ty Capel and week-ends at home.

"Caring" was a problem in those days, and as it is today, compromises had to be made. This situation was to make things easier for both uncle Owen's family and my own for a short while at least.

25

I stayed at Ty-Capel but my times were regulated in between being at home at Trem Eilian as well. I was called "Come and go" by my friends because of my travelling between the two villages.

Between my uncle and myself there was at least always someone to watch over my grandmother most of the time. All the house-work and shopping was done by her two daughters: my auntie Nell and auntie Sydney.

My family soon settled down at Brynyrefail, all four sisters attended the small village school that was totally run by Miss Parry (a lady who was to figure in my future education and entry to H.M.S. Conway). I was to attend the school at Cwm-y-Glo.

The building of the council houses at Trem Eilian made a big difference to the village of Brynyrefail. It brought families into the village and in our time there we had plenty of friends.

We had ups and downs throughout and at Trem Eilian it was not any different; the first major incident to hit the family was to hospitalise my sister Eluned, a baby at the time. As we were all getting ready for school she somehow managed to spill a cup of tea over herself, and scalded her chest. She was in hospital at Bangor for many months and when she finally came home fully recovered from the injuries, the shock had left her suffering from acute asthma. This condition was to prevail throughout our time in North Wales only to clear completely when we moved to Corby, and strangely whenever she returned to Wales on holidays or for any other visits, the condition would return.

Although it was a new council house the heating consisted of one coal fire in the living room: the kettle and teapot would always be ready near the fire and on one cold night all the family were hugging the fire and as poor Mam was trying to get things done, she knocked the teapot over. It was another disaster along the same vein, this time when Mam accidentally knocked over a teapot it was my turn: scalding my right foot very badly, my other sister Awena had slight burns but, thank God, only slight. The result of the injury was life long scarring and damage to the tendons that required treatment later in life. God bless her, she made up for it a million times over.

As it was my eleven-plus year I missed out on all my schooling prior and was unable to sit the exams, but I will come to that later.

The evening of the accident we had heavy snow, in fact at the back of the house it had drifted up to roof level. The only way in or out of the house was through the front door that was at the end of the house and sheltered. The only means of help was the St John Ambulance member who lived in the village half a mile away. I cannot remember his name but for sure he saved the day as it was several days before Doctor Douglas was able to visit.

My association with the village of Brynyrefail was a very happy one. I somehow or other got involved with the local butcher who lived nearby in a small farm called Bryn Madog, with his daughter. The house was also shared with his brother and his wife. Ioan Roberts the butcher and his daughter lived in the front of the house, his brother, Alun Roberts and his wife lived at the back.

I worked as a butcher boy for Ioan Roberts for 10 shillings a week, it was hard work but he was a fair minded man and a kind man who was very soon to become a good friend. We travelled around the villages in the butcher van. I would have to run up to small hamlets high in the hills in good and bad weather to do the deliveries. The work was rewarding: I was able to give Mam some money and to save for my first bike, but the most rewarding as far as the family was concerned was Ioan's kindness: at the end of each week anything that was left on the van he would give to me for my Mam, God bless him. We grew up healthy because of people like him.

Times were hard for my dad. Dinorwig quarry was coming to the end of it slate producing life and work was unpredictable: every bit helped.

I got to know Ioan's family very well. I would do some work for his brother Tom, who was also a butcher. His sister Maggie was also a true friend. His youngest brother Alun and his wife, auntie Beril, became special. I regarded Beril as my aunt and when she died at a young age I was shattered.

I worked as a butcher boy Friday and Saturday and on an odd Wednesday. I would deliver sausages on an old delivery bike the rest of the week. I spent quite a bit of time with Alun and auntie Beril. Alun ran the small holding at Bryn Madog and was also a dealer in livestock, mostly young calves imported from Ireland and other places. He was well known in North Wales and was seen at cattle markets most Mondays. His customers were farmers from farms isolated in the hills and attending a market for them was time consuming and costly: having a trusted dealer was a better option.

I would travel all over with Alun and we have been lifelong friends. I never missed seeing him when I returned to visit Wales. He lived to a grand old age, well over ninety years old (his great love was singing and he continued to do so to a ripe old age).

Of the many farms that I went to, two come to mind: Rhyd - y- Delin near Llangefni in Anglesey was a large cattle farm that was run by an old farmer and his sons, their milking stock were Freisians black and white cattle, with mixed store cattle. I would get the run of the yard and the barns whenever we went there. I soon came to know the dogs, and visited the milking cows when they gave birth. My favourite was the massive bull that was penned in the open at the end of the yard. He was good tempered and would tolerate a few pats and a rub.

On one visit the old farmer invited us to have a look at a new young bull they had brought in to replace the old fellow in the yard; he was in a barn and making a lot of noise, bellowing and head-butting the door: I said to Alun after how bad tempered he was.

"They are always like that when they first come in, being young and full of himself," was Alun's reply.

Our next visit was a social visit owing to an unfortunate incident. The new bull had gored the old farmer very badly, Alun went upstairs to offer his regards I remember, but his recovery was slow and I was not to see the old chap again. The farmer had entered the yard one morning with his faithful Welsh Corgi at his side without knowing that the bull was loose in the yard. Being slow of movement he was in no-mans-land and took the brunt of a charge, the bull pinned him to the ground with his knee as they normally do and managed to gore him, not badly, but the shock to an elderly man was acute. His saviour at the end of the day was the Welsh Corgi: he went for the bull's nose and was flung several yards for his trouble: this gave the farmer a moment to crawl to shelter. As we were leaving, we went into the yard to have a look at the bull, he was by now locked in the pen vacated by the former occupant. He was still red eyed and bad tempered and I was pleased to see the teeth marks on his nose.

Months went by before our next visit, and by now a lot of changes had taken place in the farm, the old farmer had passed away, the steel tubular pen was empty, the yard was void of the usual noises of dairy cattle bellowing for their calves. The sons had altered the business from dairy to store cattle, the whole place had lost its character, on our way out I thought I heard the yapping of the Corgi - maybe? Possibly maybe not?

Another farm we use to visit was mainly a sheep farm with a few cattle. The farm was situated in the most stunning area with the high mountains of Snowdonia all around, in between Cwm Penant and Cwm Strallyn (Cwm meaning valley). The farm road meandering towards the farm from the public road was three miles long - your eye could follow the road up or down the whole length to check if another vehicle was coming up or down.

The farmer and his wife were Welsh through and through, they spoke Welsh using words that you would not hear in every day use. I would be welcomed with a glass of butter-milk and a slice of bara-brith, I would then have the freedom to investigate the barns and a small field adjoining the farm building that housed the tubs (rams) when they were not with the flock. Some would have their front leg and back leg tied together with a bit of string to stop them jumping over the stone walls. I loved to see the sheep dogs and my favourite was a bitch called Bess. The farmer's wife would inform me as to what dog was at home in the barn. Sometimes Bess would be out on the hills: I would be disappointed.

When the business was done, Alun would let me drive the old Austin 20 all the way down to the public road. When I say drive, we freewheeled and he would take over at the gate and start the engine up.

On another visit I was welcomed in the usual manner, but before I could ask the farmer's wife informed me that Bess was in the barn if I wanted to go and see her. I ran over but Bess was not at her usual place, but situated in the far corner laying down on an old army great coat with a brood of new pups. I spoke to her and offered her my hand, her tail was wagging two to a dozen and she licked my hand with joy, pleased to see me and so very proud of her new pups. She was happy for me to pick up each pup, talking to her all the time, I will never forget that magic moment.

The next time we visited, Bess was at work on the hills, but one of the pups was there. His name was Gel and I was able to work him on a long lead (string) in the little field that housed the tubs, he was a natural and very enthusiastic hence the need to have him on the long lead. The tubs were none too keen, but after a while we managed to bunch them together at one end of the field. After a while it was time to go. The farmer held Gel on a short lead and as we entered the old Austin 20 he handed me the lead and said "look after him now".   I was overwhelmed. Alun drove the Austin down the farm road that day as I held on to Gel. I was not able to have Gel at home, he had to live at Bryn Madog with Mick, my other dog, but that is another story.

Before moving away from Trem Eilian, in the village of Brynyrefail, I would without doubt have to mention the kindness of the people in the village: the St John's man; Miss Parry and the Bryn Madog family; one other lady that comes to mind was Eluned Potter, she lived in Penisarwaen and on one sausage delivery day I took a tumble coming down a steep hill near to the village school. I was not hurt, just a few scrapes and bumps, but the sausages were all over the place.   Eluned's house was the first call and the next hour was spent washing the grit off the sausages and packing them up again, God bless her, we did not have one complaint from the customers. She and her brothers Gryffydd, Harry and Hugh were all good friends.

Alun Roberts was none too keen to use the veterinary surgeon because of the costs involved, but at the same time he would never see an animal suffer in any way, and as was the case with all the farmers in our area who owned one or two cows and a pig or two, money was tight.

At the same time the two cows at Bryn Madog were vital to his business as a cattle dealer. Alun's speciality were young calves and his customers were in the main small time farmers who worked as quarrymen as their day job, and using Alun's expertise to further their stock was a better option that attending the cattle market.

The milk the two cows provided was essential as most of the calves would stay at Bryn Madog overnight or for a day or two before being moved on to their new homes, and would need at least one feed.

This brings me on to another story that is embedded in my mind.

Both cows would have to visit the bull from time to time and although artificial insemination was available, only the bigger dairy farms tended to use it. A farmer nearby who had a bull was a better option, the only draw back was that the cow would have to be taken to the farm that had the bull.

That particular farmer deserves a mention; he was a rather large man, ruddy faced, who appeared to have never shaved, he never wore a jumper or a jacket, always appeared shirt-sleeved with the sleeves rolled up, he wore a very large pair of trousers that were held up by a pair of braces.

His farm was a small dairy farm. He also had sheep and pigs, and the bull gave him a little extra revenue. He was a full time small farmer you would say.

Alun Roberts as I have mentioned before had a laid back attitude to everything and whenever I arrived at Bryn Madog I could just carry on and do whatever task needed to be done. He would never leave a note or request a favour and never take me to task if I had done something off my own back, sometimes he would be at home, other times not.

I loved to take the other cow to visit the bull, she was no bother and was always good tempered. I would put a halter over her head and lead her up to the farm gate two hundred yards at a time then I would let her graze on the green grass by the road side for a bit. We would pass through the gate at the top and over the lane to cross the fields to the other farm, other animals in their fields would run around with their tails in the air when we appeared.

When I arrived at the farm gate I would tie Mick the dog to the gate post as he was not allowed in the farm yard. By this time the old bull was aware of our presence and was creating a lot of noise, head butting the half door and bellowing like mad. The cow was not bothered one bit. I held her with her back to the commotion while the farmer led the bull out of the barn. The bull made a lot of noise butting some empty buckets and sniffing the air. At last the deed was done and he was led back to the barn with his memories.

I would have to leave the cow in another barn and run back to my mother's house in Trem Eilian for my tea: I would give the cow some fresh hay, untie Mick and run for home. Mick was not allowed beyond our farm gate and was sent home, but without fail he would be there whenever I came back. How he knew I intended to return I don't know ?

After tea I would return to walk the cow home again, there would be great excitement when we returned. The little cow would run up and down beside the farm road glad to see her friend back so she could boss her about once more.

When it was the turn of the little cow the whole scenario would change, both Alun and myself would be involved. She was not keen to go and I would lead her, pulling her along by a halter over her nose, and Alun would encourage her by smacking her on the rump with his cap.

Having got going the journey was the same, Mick would be tied to the farm gate and we would enter the yard. The reaction from the bull was not the same. He made plenty of noise but was far more cautious in his approach. Alun would have tied some rope to the cow's horns, I would hold on to one and he held the other, our aim was to prevent the cow turning round. And yes, the little cow had horns while the other cow had been dehorned and yes, I think the old bull knew it as well.

Finally it was all over and the bull, rather gladly I would think, returned to the barn.

The little cow would still be in a tantrum stamping her front foot and being agitated. After the rope had been removed she would head for home in a hurry, I would run ahead to open the gate and untie Mick. Mick wasted no time in getting up to the top of the wall for safety reasons, there was never a need to lead her or encourage her, she was hell bent on getting home. She would be welcomed by the other cow in exactly the same manner.

CHAPTER 4

Gel and Mick.

Bryn Madog farm was just up the road, along the lane from my parent's house, which was called Trem Eilian, in the village of Brynyrefail. I spent most of my time there: school was not a priority to me at that time and was the reason that I did not learn a thing until much later.

The farm house was shared by the Roberts family: Ioan Roberts was a butcher and I worked as a butcher boy for him. His brother, Alun, and his wife were very soon to become my friends and I spent a lot of my time with them; they had no children. Auntie Beril, as I called Alun's wife, was unable to have children and she sadly passed away at a young age.

I was given my dog Gel by a farmer and although I was not able to have him at home he soon settled in at the farm and became Auntie Beril's dog, so much in fact that he became more attached to her than to me and to women rather than to men. He would come along to the field with me and at times his sheep dog instinct would show through but after only a short while he would head back home. He was allowed in the dairy to be with Auntie Beril while Mick was not.

Mick was Alun's dog but was also my best friend. An old dog, he had the background of an English sheep-dog - not by any means a good looking animal. Mick showed very little inclination to be indoors, the farm yard was his domain. Mick had great herding instincts no matter if they were "cats", "cattle", or "hens" and as we had no sheep those poor animals had to suffer his attentions.

The best time of the day for Mick was milking time, 6 am

and 6pm. He would start by herding the three cats into position just outside the cowshed, not that there was a need to as they would have been there anyway. He would then make for the gate at the end of the building at exactly three minutes to 6 am or pm, under the gate he would go and up the slope, by this time our two cows would be on the way to arrive at the gate again exactly 6am or pm. He was very methodical with regards to herding the two cows, he would first take a position to the left and then to the right, eventually taking a position some four yards behind the two cows and all this in the classic sheep-dog fashion. The cows did not take kindly to all this so Mick would not go too close but on the whole they had their own hierarchy that was more important.

The little cow was the oldest, black and white with long horns. She had been at the farm the longest and totally ran the proceedings, God save the other cow if she stepped out of line! At the gate the younger cow black and white also, but with no horns, had to be slightly to the rear. She would never be allowed to go first through the gate and would only enter the cow-shed after the little cow had been chained ready for milking. The little cow would enter and if Alun was there she would go directly to her pen and allow him to chain her, if it was me in charge she would stall at the door and would not budge until she was ready and when she did enter she would let me in beside her to chain her. Now you had to go to her left, the wall side, and if the mood took her she would pin me there by leaning on me, and would not let me out, until I shouted "Alun", then she would release me.

Now you may say: why not chain her by going to the right of the pen or why chain her in the first place? Not on your life! This would not be acceptable to the old cow. The chain did not do anything, but she would not give you her milk if you tried anything that was not routine, the right side had more room but would obstruct her view over her shoulder and was for keeping an eye out: looking at what the other cow was up to!

Once the old cow was in position, then the other cow would enter and as usual, never any bother what-so-ever.

Mick had to keep away while milking was going on, the three cats were allowed in. Alun usually did the milking. I would do it when he was not available. He was very aware of any spillage and would want every drop that was available. The milk was used to feed the little calves that he had brought in from the market on Monday for delivery to the customers on Tuesday to Friday; any surplus would be churned for buttermilk and butter in the dairy.

The three cats would wait in line about half a yard from the bucket: Alun would direct one spray of milk on the face of each cat, they would lick every drop and then leave the cow shed, Mick would then practise his herding skills again as they left.

Feeding young calves is an art in itself. You have to keep a very good hold of the bucket, no second chance if you let go of the bucket, you then insert two fingers in to the calf's mouth and firmly get his face into the milk. He would then, with a bit of luck, suck his share of the milk.

Anyway back to the cows. After milking the little cow had to be unchained first and she would back away, turn round and head for the open gate. The younger, bigger cow would then follow, Mick would be waiting at a safe distance to herd them up the slope before turning round for home, job done, but should you get it wrong there would be nothing but hassle.

Three afternoons in the week I would depart for my grandmother's house, Ty Capel, and cross the river. The crossing had to be undertaken at two points "rhud-fach" or "rhud fawr". They were the only shallows on that stretch of the river. Mick would always accompany me to the river's edge: he would then be sent home. He was by the way a very obedient dog and would act immediately on command, however, should he not be pleased with the command he would lay down with his nose between his front paws, a further sharper command would get him on track again.

The routine was always the same except when Auntie Beril complained that he smelled, Alun would then suggest that a bath was to be had. I would have to go to the dairy and cut a slice off the long bar of carbolic soap that was always to be had in the dairy, and with the soap in my pocket Mick and I would head for the river, although not with the usual enthusiasm. He would lay down with his head between his front paws several times on the journey down to the river, he may have been able to smell the soap or his six sense had come into play - "who knows".

On reaching the river he would lay on the bank awaiting his fate. I would take off my shoes and socks and would have to go up the bank to get him, in to the water he went head over heels. Now the carbolic soap came in to play. By the time I had finished Mick was a snow white sheep dog: two or three more plunges in the river to wash off the soap and he would be ready to be sent home. The trip home would be exactly as normal: every hundred yards he would stop and look back, over the small railway line and up the small field, he would never look back after crossing the railway line. I then made my way to my grandmother's at Ty Capel.

Every country boy has a Rabbit story, this is mine and Mick's:
Now and again I would go down to the field near the little railway line that was full of fern and bracken, the only way

in or out was a small gate at the very top (an old bedstead frame) that could be totally blocked up. I would leave one exit point at the middle of the gate, tie four bits of string to an onion net held agape with a stick and all this hidden with fern. Mick and I would then take a roundabout route to the bottom by the railway, then on command, Mick would scamper zig-zagging through the fern, and stop at the gate. He would wait there for me to arrive and without fail there would always be a rabbit in the net, sometimes two. The only draw-back was that they were always baby rabbits, not once did I manage to catch one for the pot, to Mick's disappointment I would have to let them go.

On one occasion I decided to leave school and take a different route to Bryn Madog crossing the river at the shallows towards a small village called Stabla and then up a steep path to some heathland about half a mile from the farm. On arriving at the top I would start whistling through my fingers, high pitched and also shouting on top of my voice for Mick. Without fail after a few minutes he would arrive.

This time as he came to greet me and to receive a bit of fuss, I felt a strange prescience or a feeling that was strange. I looked behind me and some ten yards away was the little old cow, head down coming at us at a full charge. I sprinted for the wall and cleared it like a high jumper. I looked for Mick but he had headed for home like a greyhound! The little cow was standing in the middle of the clearing stamping her front foot still very agitated; I realised what had happened: we had arrived just as she was giving birth and had not seen her among the bracken. I also realised that it was the dog she was concerned about and I would have probably been safe. We gave her half an hour to calm down, then locked Mick in the barn and went to pick the calf up in the tractor and trailer, by now she was as good as gold.

My time at Bryn Madog had been short but very rewarding. Looking back, a change was inevitable, but it came so very suddenly. The butcher, Ioan, decided to retire and move to Caernarfon, his sister Maggie got married and also moved to town. Alun was to buy another smallholding at Rhosisaf, a village on the Caernarfon to Pwllheli road, but the most distressing event was the death of Auntie Beril. She died following a miscarriage. She yearned for a child and would have been a great mother. Without her Bryn Madog was to lose its magic. Gel felt the loss like we did and died shortly after. Mick never settled at the new farm and my old friend also died. Alun did the best he could but to no avail.

During this time Mam had received a letter from Mr Williams, my teacher at Bryn Eryr, a church school where I had not long been in attendance. He was very worried with regards to my education. Out of the twelve or so boys at school, I was bottom of the class and to make matters worse all my good work was exactly the same as my best friend Richard Jones's, we sat together in class so it was obvious to all what was going on.

Mam was very upset and action was instant: Mam would not tolerate this but that story can be told in another chapter.

This photograph of Alun Roberts of Bryn Madog with me was taken in 2005. Alun was still driving. The photograph was taken at Rhosisaf, his home after he left Bryn Madog Farm.

This is Alun Roberts with my friend Richard Jones. Richard's father, Mr Foulks Jones, was a well known coach of male singers in the area and a native of Fachwen, as was Alun Roberts. Mr Foulks Jones was responsible for teaching Alun and many others in a lifetime of singing. Alun sang for the local Male Voice Choir for many years.

CHAPTER 5

The Slate Quarry

My home village of Cwm-y-Glo owed its existence to the numerous quarries in the area, the principle being Dinorwig Quarry in the Elidir mountain range.

The other that deserves a mention was Chwarel Glyn because of its second world war involvement. When I was growing up the quarry had stopped producing slate and all through the war years it stock-piled explosives and ammunition in its deep caverns. It is also said to have held the Crown Jewels for safe keeping, this may not have been true but when I was young it was talked about.

After the war a continuous convoy of lorries trudged their way through the village on their way to dispose of their lethal cargo in the Irish Sea.

The Thomas side of the family were from Anglesey and settled in the parish of Llanddeiniolen in 1823 at the village of Clwt-y-Bont. My grandfather, Lewis Azariah Thomas and his family lived in New Street in 1880 before his marriage to my grandmother Elizabeth Jones. Lewis Thomas was to die young and Elizabeth remarried to John Roberts.

The Jones' and Roberts' were among the first of the families to settle in the village and in my grandfather's obituary it is mentioned that he was from the village's oldest family (the Roberts Family of Bryn Ffynnon). The Jones family history mentions the epic journey my great grandmother made from Llaniestyn to Cwm-y-Glo.

My father Harry Thomas Roberts was born in 1909, the youngest son, and never knew his father Lewis Thomas, and was completely dedicated to his step father John Roberts. He started work in the quarry at the age of 14 in 1923 and left in 1955 to start a new life in Corby, Northamptonshire. Like many others from the area, they took the opportunity of new employment in the steel industry. He was to serve a five year apprenticeship as a quarryman learning the art of splitting and trimming slate. The slate would be trimmed to various sizes always referred to by the female terms, e.g. Queen, Duchess, Princess and others, the largest being the most valuable. The apprentices were made aware of the importance of the flow of the grain and any waste was not tolerated as it made no money at the end of the month.

Quarrymen were paid basic wages for the first three weeks of each month on the last Friday of each month. That was known as "cyfri mawr" - it was then that they were paid the bonus depending on how the production of good slate had gone. Most of the household bills were settled and the family men would, with a bit of luck, get some pocket money. The last Friday in the month brought some joy to the life of the quarryman. The pub in our village, the Railway Hotel (Fricsan), was the centre point and as a child I would hide behind a wall to listen to the old Welsh hymns being sung time and time again.

Ellis was the village policeman. A big fellow who had served in the first world war, he had lost a leg in the conflict. The loss made little difference to Ellis as he commanded the respect of all the village men and women.

Dinorwig quarry 1780-1969 employed 3000 men at its peak and some 300 at the time of its closure.

The finished slate product was transported by a narrow gauge railway to Port Dinorwig and then shipped to all parts by iron hulled steamers. The slate was blasted out of the cliff in an opencast mine and moved on a narrow gauge system in large pieces to galleries that would finish the slate by slitting and trimming to size. There was a time when shire horses were used in the larger galleries such as "Australia" and "Brauch", once the animal arrived he was there to stay as they would be too big to get down the steep mountain. The quarrymen took great care of them. Dinorwig Quarry was the second largest of North Wales quarries.

My father worked in a large shed segregated into small sections that they called "wall". The segregated sections ran along each side of the shed, in the middle ran the heavy machinery that machined the blocks of heavy slate to manageable sections for slitting, the noise was horrendous and the atmosphere heavy with slate dust.

My father worked alongside a colleague and an apprentice. Their work was varied: slitting, trimming and clearing up the waste material, and stacking the finished slate ready for moving at the end of each month. They were part of a squad of six men and an apprentice. Four of the men mined the slate and made sure it was transported to the shed for finishing, not an easy task as it would have to travel some distance and identification of each load was vital. The work was very heavy, carrying the heavy slabs from the tables caused many back problems.

The work at the rock face as I understand it included drilling high on the rock face then setting up the blasting. The men had to be very good rope climbers. After the blasting they would separate the good material from the scrap and load the wagons for transportation to the galleries for finishing, this was heavy work and took its toll on many.

Blasting took place three times a day and the warning

siren became part of the community way of life as each blast was carried out at exactly the right time. In the quarry itself prior warning would be given followed by the final warning. At that point everyone had to be in the shelter. The shelters were slate built with thick walls, the men would use them as a canteen (cabin) as well.

Everything with regard to tooling and electrical / engineering was carried out at the bottom or ground level near the lake, the quarry hospital was also located there. The offices, bus station and the main access to the area were also there. All the finished slate was transported by a narrow gauge railway to Port Dinorwig, this little train also became part of the everyday life in the community as it travelled a good way and through many villages. Before the buses became the normal way quarrymen went to work, my father would walk to Pen-y-Bont and use the little train to finish his journey. Edward Thomas and Harry Jones, my great-great-great grandfathers became quarrymen prior to 1800 working in small quarries around the area.

All the menfolk who followed were quarrymen without exception. At the age of twelve, my father took me to work with him one day. He had promised me that he would take me one day, I had looked forward to going for weeks and the great day came on a last Friday of the month. I was not at school as it was the summer holiday, a lovely day in July. My family had by now moved to the village of Brynyrefail. My mother was not very keen on me going as she made it very clear that I would not work there when I left school.

The old green Crossville bus arrived at the small bridge at Brynyrefail smoking like a train. All the windows were open to let out the cigarette smoke as all the men aboard smoked in those days: Woodbine, Park Drive and Turf were the chosen brands.

The short trip to the quarry bottom did not take long. On disembarking we went a little further on to the tally station to pick up our tally: a square brass disc with a number on it. Further on again to the first incline, the incline was steep with small wooden carriages going up and others descending, the weight of the carriages descending pulling the upwards carriages up the incline. The operator had to be very aware of the many problems that could occur, the balance had to be right and the speed and the travel had to be regulated using the brake.

We all clambered on: if there was too many some would have to get off and the same at the top, some of the men would get off before it came to a stand still. At the top, the wire rope would wind round a big drum operated by an electric motor. To arrive at my father's place of work we had to take three rides on the inclines. On arrival we deposited our tally in the tally station, our numbers had been marked on a board and a nail had been hammered above the number to hand the tally on.

My father worked at the first section as you entered the shed, everything would have been left as it was the day before, work would begin immediately and under the direction of Douglas the apprentice I made myself useful. He also showed me round and introduced me to the men who worked nearby. One man in particular stood out as a character, his name was Richard Jones and he went by the name of Dick–the–feet to all the men who knew him. Richard walked in a peculiar way with his feet splayed out like a duck, it was said that this was caused by carrying the very heavy slate slaps and lifting them on to the table. Richard was very well thought of and respected by his fellow workers, he was also a friendly and open man.

The way the system worked is hard to understand: Richard Jones worked completely on his own while my father worked within a squad of seven. The section my father worked in had ample room, while the section next door was small and narrow. Richard worked there, and I will attempt to describe his method of making a living. In a way he could be described as a scavenger as he took the scrap and off-cuts that others would have thrown away, he would manage to produce the smaller versions of the finished roofing slate and having only to make a living for himself managed to survive.

At around 8.30 a.m. my father and Douglas the apprentice went over to the canteen (cabin) for their morning break. They took it in turns, as the work never stopped. The canteen was a big building with tables along both sides, a large wood burning stove in the middle, and the hot water boilers for the tea next to the stove. I sat between my father and Douglas, all the men brought out their snap boxes. My father's box I knew very well having a round end and a square end the two portions fitting in to one another, he would have had bread and jam or bread and corn-beef, possibly a boiled egg, and some cake (Bara-Brith), some of the men had red Oxo tins, the name printed on the lid.

The men started to eat and drink their tea all conversing and taking no notice of me, I felt a bit embarrassed as I had nothing and Dad was taking no notice. After a few minutes and quite suddenly one of the men looked to my direction and pointed a finger, he uttered so everyone could hear "who have we here and what is your name?" I lowered my head down as I gave him my name, he then turned to my dad and asked why I did not have a "snap'. My father said nothing.

One of the other men took over and said "we can not have this."

Douglas somehow or other brought out a spare lunch box that was passed around the table and I finished with a box full of goodies as each man gave me an item from their snap-box. I realised now that it was planned but as a child of twelve I was overwhelmed by their kindness.

The men left the table one by one, they all left their lunch boxes where they sat. I took an apple from my box and walked over to the stable to visit the two massive horses that lived there. They were not working on the day I was there. I cut my apple in half with a bit of slate and gave them half each.

I had another look around before returning to clean up and make myself useful. I also cleaned up Richard Jones' area while he went for his break.

The time went very quickly and the afternoon was soon upon us and another surprise and an event that has stayed with me all my days. We left our section heading for the canteen for what I thought was our dinner break. The only difference was that everyone was going and the working places had been left clean and tidy for the Monday morning. We sat in the same place and finished off our snap. After a while someone started singing at the other end of the canteen. The good tenor voice was soon joined by others. I was baffled by all this and by now there was only standing room left in the canteen.

The singing continued for some time. Everyone who was not eating was singing. At long last one of the men took a position in the middle near the tea urns and announced the retirement of a fellow quarryman, he gave a brief history and asked the man to join him.

By this time I had spotted the man who was retiring. The man in question look very uncomfortable and apprehensive, however he walked up to join his colleague and was asked to say a few words. He brought out a piece of paper from his waistcoat pocket and started to speak. He had only said a few words before he was interrupted by a well wisher who came out of the crowd to shake his hand. He started all over again but after a few moments he was again interrupted. This went on several times. He had his hand shaken and he was hugged by others, he never did finish his words of thanks. Needless to say, he was showing the strain and emotion by this time. To break the proceedings up, the tenor at the back started singing again and was joined by all his mates, they seemed to pick the saddest songs. With men departing and making their way to the inclines for a ride down the canteen choir finished with the old choir song "Myfanwy".

The down trip on the inclines was less busy as some of the younger men just ran down to make up time.

Many years have gone by since I remembered this story, my father has long gone having retired at the age of 65 from the steel industry, I myself retired at 58 and today people make nothing of a retirement.

In 1952 it was completely different, the men who did retire would be 70 and older. There would be no pension for a quarryman and only the few lived that long; lung diseases and problems similar to the coal miners, cut short their life span. Now being older and possibly wiser, I understand the reason for such celebrations.

51

Photographs of the quarry as it is now in 2015, many
years after it closed down.

CHAPTER 6

Miss Parry

Having lived a childhood of complete freedom and not a care in the world and in the most wonderful part of Wales, void of the concerns that today's parents have to worry about, I was free to enjoy the rural life. At the same time respect for the elderly and good manners was instilled into us all.

Suddenly I was thrown into the real world when Mam received a letter from Williams expressing concern regarding my progress at school. I had not been at Bryn Eryr long, having missed out on my eleven-plus examination because of a serious injury to my right foot, as mentioned in Chapter 3. I was bottom of the class.

Bryn Eryr was an old church school with twelve or so boys, the girls class was at the same school under the charge of a Miss Owen, but boys and girls were taught separately. Williams thought that if I was to pay more attention to learning I did have the potential. Mam was not the cleverest person in the world, but at the same time she was not the sort to stand for this kind of nonsense and took the matter into her own hands.

I came home one day to be firmly informed that as from that moment I would be under charge of Miss Parry and would attend her house three times a week for tuition. Miss Parry was the schoolmistress at the small village school at Brynyrefail, a middle aged lady very respected by all the villagers. My Mam had somehow managed the arrangement free of charge provided that I was fully committed. Mam knew Miss Parry very well as my four sisters attended the small school that she dominated. The arrangement was to change my life and turn things round

53

once again.

I was to keep my butcher boy job until Ioan Roberts retired. This provided the money that I would have to save for another project Mam had in hand. I will come to that later.

On my first visit to Miss Parry she gave me a pencil, rubber and a pencil sharpener as well as providing writing paper, she spoke to me as an adult and made no bones as regard to the hard work ahead and that she tolerated no nonsense. After a few weeks I began to improve and with the improvement my confidence also improved. At the start I could not converse in English "having never had to". I found it very hard but Miss Parry would only teach in English. I could manage the two times table but not the others.

She found the whole thing a challenge, like a football manager with a must-win attitude. As the weeks went by I think she was more up for it than I was.

This went on for a time until a change in direction was necessary. Mam had somehow found out about a vacancy for a place at H.M.S Conway in Anglesey for one boy from Caernarfonshire and one from Anglesey, (both were Welsh counties at that time). This was available under a sponsorship scheme run by the education department.

Mam pestered that department until they put me on the list and even after she would ask her friends to go to the department office to attain some news or any further information. She finally managed to have my name put on the list but was firmly reminded that an entrance examination had to be undertaken before entry and that only the top marked boy would get the vacancy.

I continued my lessons with Miss Parry and made steady progress. My work at school was also showing the same improvement and Williams was impressed. At this point I should mention that Williams was a firm no nonsense teacher who was very well liked by his pupils. At the time and for many years after his popularity was well known. He was a former Royal Navy officer who had served throughout the Second world war, and a noted boxer.

Many years after I had moved away from North Wales, my friend Richard Jones and I would visit Williams at the pub that was his regular. Whenever I returned home on holiday, he would converse and never forgot one boy that went through his hands at Bryn Eryr.

I turned up for one particular lesson with Miss Parry to be shown a set of entry examination papers for H.M.S. Conway for the previous year's intake, questions and answers. Later on, she also obtained old eleven-plus papers that we studied thoroughly, examination procedures she insisted that I knew off by heart and her insistence paid off later.

As time went on a date was set for the entry examination for H.M.S. Conway and to everybody's surprise I was to also re-sit my eleven plus. This was not expected as it was felt that one examination was more than I should undertake and the H.M.S. Conway was to be my priority, however Miss Parry felt that it would do no harm to have a go.

The venue was at the old Grammar School at Brynyrefail over the road from the old chapel. Miss Parry's little school was just behind the chapel and her home a bit further down the road, half a mile away was Mam's house at Trem Eilian.

The H.M.S. Conway examination was to be in the morning, the eleven-plus in the afternoon. Many days of hard work were to follow. The apprehension was terrible, how I coped with it I do not know.

The big day came round sooner than I expected. The apprehension was catching, Mam and Miss Parry were as bad as I was. I was to be in the foyer of the grammar school at 8.45 am, a Mr So-and-so would then direct and accompany me to an empty class-room. I was assured that he would look after my needs.

The foyer was full of children, one or two that I knew, the majority I did not as the catchment area for the grammar school covered a very wide area and many villages. They all had their school uniform on, both the boys and girls, all the boys in long trousers. I felt out of place - the short trousers that I wore did not help. None of the children paid any attention to me, and thank the Lord, for had one child made one remark I would have disintegrated altogether.

I sat on a desk at the front of the empty classroom: a pencil, a pencil sharpener and a rubber were provided, the examination paper was also at the ready. Mr So-and-so sat at the teacher's desk in front of me with a timer that would ring when he struck the top. No other person was in the room.

I started well answering the first three questions with ease then turned the page and was surprised that as I went on the questions were very familiar and it did not take me long to realise that the paper was exactly the same as the sample paper Miss Parry had provided at my lessons. Nevertheless I continued through the paper then rechecked my spelling, full-stops and commas. The second and third times I went through the paper I made sure that I had not missed anything.

When Mr So-and-so rang the bell contraption to stop the

time I nearly jumped out of my skin, he then came over and placed the examination papers in an envelope which was then sealed and stamped.

I made no comment or mention with regard to the paper being familiar. I was then free to go to lunch. I ran home for a cup of tea and bread and jam. Mam was keen to know how I had progressed but I still made no mention about the familiarity of the examination papers.

When I arrived back Mr So-and-so and Miss Parry were waiting for me at the foyer, Miss Parry just asked if I was "ok" before I was led back to the same desk as before. This time there were two more children taking the examination and two adults seated near to the window. I was later to learn that the two other children had missed their eleven plus examination through a serious illness called infantile paralysis (polio) and that the two adults were carers.

My approach to the procedure was the same; go through the paper first time and answer what I could, the second time answer the questions that I had missed the best I could, but to make sure that some kind of an answer was given, the third time check spellings, full-stops and commas. The next paper was arithmetic: I did the best I could.

The second part of the examination was to write an essay, a choice of three subjects that related to our area. The one I chose was "sheep farming". I cannot remember what the other two were, but I am more than sure I would not have considered them anyway as "sheep farming" suited me very well.

I wrote about my old friend, Mick the sheep dog, and changed his exploits with the cows and cats at Bryn Madog to an imaginary sheep farm in the hills. I was so in my element writing about such a familiar topic that I nearly failed to bring it to a conclusion when Mr So-and-so stopped the proceedings to inform us that only five more minutes would be allowed thus allowing me the necessary time.   At the end the papers were inserted in a brown envelope and sealed. I was then free to go home, in the evening I was sent over to thank Miss Parry.

I never mentioned the H.M.S. Conway papers to her, I did worry about it but did not want to make a fool of myself.

Having all this behind me I found that I had more time, school work was never a problem any more, I was comfortable and more confident. I continued working as a butcher boy and my presence at my grandmother's was as important as ever.

A few weeks passed by and as ever they brought changes. The results of the H.M.S. Conway examination were positive and I was awarded a place at the naval college at Plas Newydd in Anglesey for a period of just under two years. My fellow student was to be a William Roberts of Amlwch, Anglesey. The sponsorship awarded by the Caernarfonshire Education Board covered most of the major costs: uniform was to be provided by the college but all other items like shirts, shoes and sport items, Mam had to find the money to buy.

I had worked as a butcher boy for a period of time and the amount saved up was very useful as a major change was being planned by my mother: a move to Corby in Northamptonshire. My dad had already moved there to work in the Tube Works "but that is another story".

I also received help from other sources, family friends and the Roberts family of Bryn Madog.

My mother received a list of items and a programme of the events was to follow.   The list of items I had to have was something like this:

Three pairs of black socks.
Three pairs of underpants.
One pair of black dress shoes.
One pair of plimsolls.
White handkerchiefs.
One pair of shorts.
Three white vests.
A black tie.
Three Van Heusen collar-less shirts and three collars
A pair of pyjamas
Tooth-paste and a tooth brush and a comb.

There may have been more items on the list.   I would also take with me my everyday items.

I had never worn underpants;   toothpaste and tooth brushes were not in use in my family; one comb was used by us all; I had one pair of shoes; handkerchiefs were only used by rich people; and I had never heard of plimsolls! It seemed as if I was to join the upper class.

I was also to have a suitcase. This was no problem as one was found in my grandmother's house.   My initials J.C.T. were to be printed on the front.   That old suitcase went all over the world with me and I still have it to this day in the attic gathering dust.

Shortly after, my mother had a visit from Mr So-and-so. He had I'm sure been in touch with Miss Parry. The gist of the visit was as follows: I had to everyone's surprise been awarded a pass in the eleven-plus examination, the pass was at the very lowest end, and he was there to offer my mother some advice.

The advice was really not necessary as my mother was adamant that I was to go to H.M.S. Conway. Should I have gone to the grammar school it was felt that it would be a burden on the family and also on myself as I would have been well behind the others in my age group, in fact I would be one year behind, and with my pass it would be very hard for me to catch up. His advice was that I took the opportunity to go to the naval college.

With all that now behind me the next event was my entry to H.M.S. Conway at Plas Newydd near to the village with the long Welsh name shortened to Llanfair P.G.

HMS Conway sinking

The original sailship of HMS Conway needed to go for a re-fit in Birkenhead in 1953. Local pilots for the Menai Straits advised the crew that 3 tugs should be used instead of just 2 as in 1949 when the ship had arrived from Birkenhead, but their warnings were ignored. As the ship approached the suspension bridge an unexpected strong current made the boat uncontrollable and the near tug was moved to the front in an effort to control the ship. This left the rear uncontrolled and also lost valuable time. Minutes later HMS Conway ran aground on flat rocks near the bridge. As the tide went down the ship's back broke, leaving her wrecked on the edge of the Straits.

The wreck was left until 1958 when Caernarfon Harbour Board began work on removing the wreck. However, during the work the boat caught fire and was burnt down to water level. The remains of the boat can still be seen at low tide.

The school was still housed on the side of Plas Newydd for a further 20 years. During this time tents borrowed from the Army were used while more huts were constructed. The school finally closed in 1974 when funding was withdrawn. During its final time in Plas Newydd both Ian Duncan Smith and Sir Clive Woodward studied at HMS Conway.

This information and picture is from the HMS Conway website.

CHAPTER 7

H.M.S. Conway

H.M.S. Conway was a naval college situated in the grounds of Plas Newydd the home of the Marquis of Anglesey. The area is the most beautiful part of Anglesey near to the shores of the Menai Straits, the view further into Caernarfonshire exposes the panorama of the distant Welsh mountains.

The family of the Marquis was still in residence, the best part of the house having been converted to accommodate the college, with shore establishment for further use. The area included a small harbour, woodland, coastal area and plenty of green fields. The out of bound areas were clearly marked out, but on the whole we had plenty of freedom to enjoy the facilities.

I had been awarded a scholarship by the Caernarfonshire Education Board for a two year stay that would finally allowed me to enter the merchant navy as an apprentice engineer. Anglesey in those days was a separate county and would also have one scholarship boy. In my time there, the other lad was William Roberts from Amlwch.

The college had moved during the second world war from the Mersey-side area for safety reasons and before my time there was based on an old vessel that would be moored on the Menai Straits. I remember her very well as she went aground just under the Menai Suspension bridge and was a tourist attraction for a long time. She had been renamed H.M.S. Conway from her former name of H.M.S. Nile. I would cycle as a youngster to view the ship and the attempts to make her sea-worthy once again. She was finally set alight and disposed of that way. I was not to know at that time that I would be involved at the college for nearly two years.

I left my former school Bryn Eryr at the end of the summer term shortly after my 14th birthday and for the love of me I have no recollections of the day I entered H.M.S. Conway, who if anyone took me there or if I went by bus or who was I to contact on my arrival, in fact the first two weeks there are completely blank.

William Roberts may have played a part in all this as he was a completely different lad to me, full of confidence and outgoing and possibly under his leadership I made it through the initial period.

When I did finally settle down we went our different ways and were not close. William was from a seafaring family, fully committed to being a naval officer and would go on to serve on deep-sea vessels for many years followed by service on the Irish ferries at Holyhead, he was finally made coxswain of the famous Moelfre lifeboat. It was there that I last met up with him. The same lifeboat was made famous in the early days of television for its bravery and heroic rescues, the then coxswain being awarded the highest acclaim possible.

I was installed in a large dormitory named after the Cunard liner "Mauritania". My bed was the last bed, next to the wall. A small cupboard was next to it for my belongings, there was also room for my suitcase underneath the bed. At the far end near to the door was a list of all the occupants, and the marks that you earned for your house were included daily against your name, and this was a very important part of life day by day at H.M.S. Conway.

After three weeks I started to settle down and I realised that I could hold my own in the classroom and the strict regimen suited me, I went with the flow and soon got on

63

with my fellow cadets.

The senior cadet of my dormitory was an 18 year old Welsh lad called Dargie. His parents owned shops and stores around the Welsh coast towns. He was not Welsh speaking but was fair and just as a senior cadet and certainly not like some of the others. His next in line was an Indian prince called Java, he would take over at some point as senior cadet as and when Dargie left, he was also fair and a gentleman, he spoke in a very posh accent. Both were very good boxers, cricket players and rugby players.

Over the first few weeks I became accustomed to the routine. The system was straight forward: it was run by officers and teachers on equal standing. Some would reside and others would live near by, the uniformed officers were in charge of everything outside the class-rooms with a lot of help from the senior cadets. Of the teachers I remember two very well, a Mr Jessup who lived with his wife in Menai Bridge, he would invite some of us for coffee evenings at his house sometimes. The other was a Mr Stringer; he was the head of our table at mealtimes in the dining hall, I remember him because of his notoriously slow eating. The rules were that only when he had finished his course could the boys start the next. He would chew for ages and take a lengthy stop between courses. We were always the last table out of the dinning hall, this shortened the time between end of meal to the start of the next activity.

A loudspeaker system was in operation throughout the day from "wakey wakey, rise and shine" first thing in the morning until "lights out". All instructions were given via the loudspeaker.

Evening activities were plentifull, We would watch boxing tournaments in our free time, and special traditional tasks were put on where you had to participate in at least one. I chose "hair dressing" for what reason I do not know, but it brings me on to another story:

Should you turn up late for class or for any activity you would be taken to task, the senior cadet decided on your punishment. Anglesey leave was usually allowed at the end of term and in my case I would be allowed to go home Friday to Sunday evening. I had to report back by 9.p.m. on Sunday. Anglesey leave would mean other things to other cadets such as parents visiting.

I would catch the Newborough to Bangor service bus at the gate, change at Bangor for the Caernarfon bus, and another at Caernarfon to Cwm-y-Glo. It was very time consuming.

The story involves all this: I went to a hair dressing class one evening and the barber that took the class right out of the blue came over to speak to me. This was rather unusual. He had never once spoken to me before and in Welsh he asked if I was due some Anglesey leave. I said that I was going home on Friday, he then offered me the use of his bike and should I want to use it I could. The barber was a local man from the nearby village of Llanfair P.G. The bike was kept in the coke bunker storage area near to the boilers covered in old sacking.

Friday came along and I checked out the coke bunker and the bike was there. An old thing that had seen better days, anyway a clean up and a drop of oil and I was away, in fact, I used it several times as I gained a lot of time travelling therefore more time at home.

One Sunday evening I was riding the bike along the A5 main road having crossed the Menai bridge and up the hill towards the village of Llanfair P.G. when I was confronted by a group of youngsters standing about at the old toll house that separated the A5 going forward towards Holyhead and the left coast road going towards Plas Newydd, Llanddaniel and Newborough. Nothing nasty just a bit of banter, I went over to them and the minute they realised that I was Welsh and spoke Welsh to them I was soon accepted. I must have been there half an hour or so, no more as I had to report in at 9 pm.

I was getting on like a house on fire with one girl and before departing managed to get a kiss or two, I thought no more of this and by the time the next hairdressing lesson came along I had totally forgotten all about it. I had not been in the classroom a minute when I was confronted by the barber and in a no nonsense manner he warned me to leave his daughter alone. I was frightened to death and for some time worried about it, unduly thank God as he never mentioned it again. Needless to say the old bike was not available the next time round.

The house system where you earned marks or points for all kind of activities was an important part of life and from time to time the list of points against your name at the back of the dormitory door was updated. Sport was the main point earner and at the time was not high on my list in term of ability.

Cricket and rugby were the two top team games, boxing was also high on the list, but there were many other sports like sailing, hockey, table tennis and others. At times the college would hold an athletic gala were everyone had to participate and if you did not sign up for one or two events they would do it for you.

At this point I had not won a point and was often reminded by the senior cadet, but things were just about to change. Purely by accident, one day I noticed that my name had been included in the cross country team. I had never been involved in any form of running and wondered what it was all about. I was told that you had to run a three mile course first through a field, then through woodlands and then along the beach before returning to the start. You could win points by winning the race or by being placed and also gain points by winning your age group; it would be the first time I would use my plimsolls.

I was not unduly concerned as all the boys that were not very good at other sports would be involved so I was in good company. On the day of the race we lined up ready for the mass start. I was near the front not by anything more than by chance: off we went, everyone showing off at the start in front of crowd that was taking the "mick". Once we had left the playing field the pace started to slow down and when we came into the woodland I was having no difficulty in being at the front. On entering the woodlands a number of the runners at the front disappeared into the bushes. I was surprised and unsure at what was happening. The runner next to me soon put me right and said that they were having a cigarette and that it was normal, but I was not to mention it to anyone. I carried on and found the rest of the opposition none too keen to make a race of it, I was pleased to win the race at a canter.

Nothing was ever mentioned, no well done or anything whatsoever. I kept looking at the list to see if I had been awarded some points for my house and after a while when I thought that they had forgotten about it I was given points for winning the race and for winning my age category. A good day's work I thought.

The next time the race was held my name was again included and everything seemed to be the same: off we went but as soon as we were out of sight of the start I was getting kicked and spat at from behind. I was tripped several times and consequently found myself well back in the field. When we reached the woodlands the same thing happened again, off they went for a cigarette. I gave this a bit of thought and realised that I had the choice of making an effort or just finishing the race. Head down I was soon alongside the leader, a lad who was older than me, possibly around 17 years old. We ran together along the beach but when we reached the playing fields he was too strong, my second place and winning my category improved my house-marks no end.

I decided to do a bit of training prior to the next race, running in the sand dunes out of sight and it paid off. The third and fourth races I was unhindered having decided to run from the front right from the start. My fourth race was also my last and behold I did get one or two "well done's". My cross country experience has stood me in good stead throughout my life as a life long runner.

Having been very fortunate to gain sponsorship for H.M.S.Conway I will always be thankful for the way I was received, I never was made to feel inept or made to feel lesser in any way to any of the others.

We had what was said to be an old war time German motor torpedo boat called "Pinner" which, under strict supervision, we used on the dangerous Menai straits, and I was included to crew the boat once or twice, also on one occasion I went to Holyhead for navigation training on the British Rail ferry, the Hibernian, crossing the Irish Sea to Cork.

The only time I was made to feel a bit peeved was (and it is a funny story rather than a serious one), in the Welsh language there is an old saying regarding the people of Anglesey being agricultural and a rough translation would be "the pigs of Anglesey" (Moch Mon). Somehow some of the boys had got to hear about this and behind my back they would utter a pig grunting. When I turned round they just had a good giggle. I did not react but laughed with them and they soon forgot all about it.

My time at Plas Newydd was coming to an end. I had already applied to join the Port Line Shipping Company and had been accepted. The end of my stay came very suddenly. I was called to the bursar's office one morning and informed that all my papers were ready for my departure the following day, I was to pack my belongings and return my uniform in the morning.

I should say at this point that I was well drilled as to the procedures of travelling, how to join the ship and who to see, how to order a taxi, and most important what not to do and who to seek information from should I need to.

My package included my pay-book, passport, some cash, and a train warrant from Bangor station to London also a pass to enter King George V dock. Times and dates and other papers: there may have been more? I was to make sure that my papers were kept in a safe place and to see the chief steward when I boarded the ship.

The lady secretary gave me the timetable for the local bus from just outside the main gate that would take me to Bangor. I would then make my way home for a few days before I set out on the next trip to the unknown.

I left without anyone wishing me well or saying goodbye, as I walked to the gate not one person acknowledged me: My time there had been invaluable, I had grown up. Thanks, Mam.

CHAPTER 8

M V Port Fremantle

After a few days at home it was time to move on to the next stage and an important time in my life. Having been away from home at the naval college, the apprehension and worry were not there and I was looking forward to the adventure.

Dad had arranged for me to travel to Bangor station with a friend of his, Tommy Hughes. I would have sooner travelled on my own and with my own thoughts, but my dad meant well so in the company of Tommy I set off on a trip that was to be a great adventure.

Tommy was a dour and silent man who had worked as a fitter at Bangor station. He had never travelled further than the station engineering shop and had he been inclined to give me advice it would I am sure be of no assistance, but he did not and never uttered more that two words the whole of the journey, and when we arrived at the station I felt a great relief when we went our different ways. The only good thing that came out of it was that somehow or other I never had to pay for the bus journey.

The next stage was the train journey to London. It was my first time on a train and the Irish Mail at that. I was elated. A great experience and the memory has stayed with me for the last sixty years. I was to take a taxi to King George V Docks. I had been well versed at the college on how to order a taxi: I should first get the cost of the fare. I remember very well asking the driver and at the same time informing him that I could not give him a tip as I was short of money. He took a long look at me and said: "Get in."

At the dock gate with my pass in my hand, I passed through. The security man never even looked my way. I knew that the ships of the Port Line Shipping Company all had red funnels, so it was not very long until I came across the Port Fremantle. She was to be my home for the next fifteen months.

The gangway was down and I could see an officer at the top. I staggered up and was confronted by a lad not a lot older than myself. We were to become very good friends. He was the senior cadet and would be the seventh officer on his next trip, a Londoner by the name of John Dixon. John was to advise and share his own experiences with me, but firstly he showed me to my cabin on the starboard side amid ship adjacent to the engine room.

71

I could see that I was to share the cabin as soon as I entered as the bottom bunk was cluttered with somebody's belongings, so I decided to wait. After a while another lad, about my age, came in. He was small but well built and already shaving while I was well away from needing to do such a deed. His name was Thompson and for the love of me, I cannot remember his first name. We became friends from the start. A nicer lad you could never meet. He was from Swaffham in Suffolk and was brought up along with his brother at a Doctor Barnados Home. He had already done one trip as a junior cadet and his next trip would be his first as an apprentice engineer. We sorted out the sharing the cabin and he then showed me round the ship.

Thompson provided me with yet another experience. He was a dedicated Roman Catholic and his brother was a priest and as my own background was, as most Welsh lads of my time, a Methodist, having been baptised and confirmed but nothing as intense as was my new friend's religious upbringing. He would say his prayers morning and evening, deep in thoughts on his knees, and would continue crossing himself at any given moment. I had never seen anything like it but like everything else in life, you get used to it.

After a while he would show me the letters his brother sent almost every week. The letters were full of instructions all deeply ingrained towards their beliefs. I often wonder how Thompson survived: did he stay at sea; did he ever get married; did he ever meet a girl even? Who knows? We were never in close contact after the first few weeks. He was in the engine room whilst I was mostly involved in learning seamanship, but certainly in all the time that I was to know him he never went home or mentioned any relations other than his brother. The ship was his new home.

The MV Port Fremantle was the oldest ship in the Port Line fleet, having seen war time service and conversion from coal burning to oil. She was built in 1927 by Workman, Clark & Co at Belfast with a tonnage of 8072 with a speed of 15 knots and having served a total of 31 years and surviving the second world war, she was finally broken up at Osaka in Japan during September 1960.

When I joined her, she had just completed a six month trip and was off-loading her cargo of frozen Canterbury (NZ) lamb at different ports. The normal crew had been paid off with the exception of John Dixon and Thompson. Dixon would take his leave later before re joining the ship for her next trip.

To cater for the off-loading and the short trips a skeleton crew were under the command of an old and possibly an ex-captain called Mr Smith. I was to have very little contact with Mr Smith or any of the crew, in fact, I was not given any instructions or acknowledged in any way. I just had to keep myself occupied and depended on John Dixon for advice.

We soon completed the off-loading in London and our next port of call was Avonmouth, near the city of Bristol. Nothing of great interest happened. The minute we tied up the crew just disappeared, including Mr Smith. When they reappeared a few days after, most of them were the worse for wear and none had any intention of doing any work. The next stage was to improve slightly: our next port of call was Rotterdam.

Rotterdam was my first visit to a foreign country. The usual exodus of the crew did not materialise this time. Thompson and I had the freedom to do what we wanted and made the most of it. We went shopping and I brought gifts for my Mam and Dad and sisters. My dad's gift was a

Philoshave electric razor and it was to be a big surprise for him as I knew my dad had never heard of an electric razor, never mind owning one. I was never able to give any of them their gifts, but I will come to that later.

Whist walking round the city we noticed that the cinema was showing the film "Rock Around The Clock" and knowing the great excitement that the advent of rock and roll were causing world wide we brought tickets.

What a wonderful night we had. The first film was "Lady Killers" and can you imagine Peter Sellers and his fellow actors speaking in Dutch as the film was dubbed over with English sub-titles. The second film was "Rock Around The Clock" with Bill Halley and the Comets. The place went mad, the Dutch kids danced on the seats and down the aisles. There was no nastiness, just great fun. Both Thompson and myself were just as carried away as they were. The whole film was again Dutch, dubbed over with English sub-titles, but it made no difference. The memory will last with me for ever.

We returned to the ship still jiving away. The ship sailed on the tide the following morning, bound for Hamburg in Germany. It was to be the last port of call. We arrived in Hamburg mid-morning and viewed the war time devastation along the shore line as we moved towards our berth. One particular area that housed submarines sticks in my mind: the thick concrete pens were caved in and some damaged submarines were still there. Not a lot more to remember about Hamburg – the whole city was teaming with service men and women.

We did visit the red light area out of curiosity but were not that impressed or interested. We noticed that all the soldiers that we spoke to were headed for a big boxing match which was to happen that night, so we joined them.

We had no money but somehow or other we managed to get in. The show started with wrestling bouts that were followed by the main event: Randy Turpin the ex-middleweight world champion fighting a German light heavyweight champion who looked massive in comparison to Turpin. The fight was very one sided and Turpin was well beaten, in fact he did not seem to have the will to make a fight of it. The whole place erupted with chairs being thrown about. We departed as soon as we could but did not feel too disappointed as we had got in free.

We were on our way again. The ship was now light in the water and rolling like mad, we were headed for the river Tyne in County Durham.

CHAPTER 9

Hawthorn Leslie Shipyard, Hebburn, Newcastle, UK

The M.V. Port Fremantle had anchored mid stream on the river Tyne, Hawthorn Leslie shipyard on one bank and Swan Hunter shipyard on the other. Further down from Hawthorn Leslie was the Naval Yard and down river Jarrow and then South Shields.

The shipyard personnel had already boarded the vessel in preparation for dry- docking at high water. The plans were that she would undergo a re-fit before undertaking her next trip and the stories circulating were that it would be a thirteen month trip, and her last voyage.

I enjoyed the procedure and seamanship in turning the vessel round and slowly nudging her into the flooded basin, and the method of ensuring that she was kept upright inside the dry-dock. When it was completed and the basin was drained the workers wasted no time. The ship was completely taken over by carpenters, painters, engineers, and all kinds of trade people.

Hawthorn Leslie was situated in Hebburn-on-Tyne, access to the yard was by a massive door with a small door in the middle (similar to a prison door) always manned by a security man. The road leading to the entrance was on a hill that led down to the ferry that crossed the river to a point near to the Swan Hunter shipyard. Opposite to the yard entrance was an old church: another road ran the other way towards the fish and chips shop that were to be our salvation during our time at Hawthorn Leslie.

The town centre and Metro station were within twenty minutes walk away. The temporary crew departed within minutes and John Dixon was also due his leave, before he went he instructed both Thompson and myself to remove all our belongings from our cabin to the safety of the chief stewards office. We complied by packing our few possessions but decided to leave a few items of clothing such as underwear in one drawer for everyday use, unfortunately I left the gifts that I had bought in Rotterdam in among my clothing. On our return to our cabin we found all we had left had been stolen. I reported this to John Dixon but all he could say was: "I told you to clear everything out".

This meant that we had no change of underwear and no money to buy any. Mr Smith had disappeared along with the rest of the crew just leaving one or two displaced persons and a cook who was always under the influence of drink to care for our needs.

Thompson could have gone home, but there was not a home for him to go to. His brother was at a catholic training college and possibly having left the Doctor Barnados home that he was brought up at, he had severed the connection. I had to stay as I had no leave to take, and no money to even buy food. Anyway we decided to make the most of the situation. I was completely dejected and making a career in the merchant navy was beginning to look like a bad idea.

After a couple of days we both decided to go out for a walk to Hebburn. We had to go on an afternoon as we had learned that leaving the sanctuary of the yard in the evening was a chancy affair: the local youths, both boys and girls, went about in gangs and should you be spotted they would chase you and beat you up.

On leaving the yard, the security man came out of his office to unlock the little door. He was an elderly man with pure white hair. There were others but he seemed to be the one that stood out. In the usual friendly Geordie way he asked: "where are you going, bonny lads?" In no time I had told him of our misadventure before continuing on our way.

A few days went by before we ventured out again and as we passed the security office by the gate a lady came out and called us over. She handed us both an envelope and inside was a five pound note. Needless to say we were baffled and flabbergasted. She explained that they had made a small collection on our behalf and that we were not to mention it to anyone. I suspected that the white haired security man had instigated the kind deed, and would have liked to thank him but every time I came across him he had a very stern and unapproachable look about him.

Across from the main gate a street led on to a fish and chip shop that was our main source of nourishment at the time. Along with the owner there were two ladies who took care of the customers and we had got to know them very well.

We would only have the money if I had managed to save the three pence the ferryman had not charged me on my daily morning trip to Swan Hunters to deliver documents and news papers. He would now and again take the three pence fare to keep me on my toes, but most of the time I had a free ride.

One day when the fish shop owner was not about one of the ladies chased after us and gave both of us a six penny piece. She uttered "come back later on bonny lads" and rushed back into the shop.

We wasted as much time as we could before going back and by this time the owner was back. We ordered our bag of chips and the lady as normal topped the bag with batter-bits. We handed over our six penny bit and was given two pence change. When we went out of the shop to enjoy our feast, I notice that our change consisted of two pence and the return of the six penny bit, and this became the routine from then on.

I will always remember the kindness of the Tyne-siders: the ferry man, the Security man, the Fish and Chips shop ladies. We never went hungry because of their generosity. The temporary crew that should have taken care of us to a certain degree, were either drunk or away.

Another time Thompson and myself, feeling sorry for ourselves, decided to walk up to Hebburn and walking by the Conservative Club towards the Metro station we notice a lady washing the steps leading in the club's front entrance and as they always do she shouted over "Where are you going bonny lads?" I went over and feeling a bit dejected and if anyone was willing to listen, gave her my tale of woe. The lady without any hesitation said "Wait there bonny lad" and went inside to reappear with a gentleman in a suit and a badge on his lapel proclaiming that he was the chairman. He asked us in and led us to the snooker table, gave us a six penny bit for the electric meter and told us to be careful that we did not damage the baize covered table. We had never played snooker and were at a loss about how to the set the balls up. Noticing our plight the barman came over to start us off: once started there was stopping us.

We were allowed in any afternoon and found the place a refuge, the kindness of the Geordie folk was never ending.

The re-fit was near to completion, but you would never have thought so with debris all over the place. Some of the temporary crew had come back, Mr Smith included, and also one or two of the permanent crew for the forthcoming voyage. My stay at Hawthorn Leslie was coming to an end, but not before the highlight of my time there. I have always been a football fan: not any team especially, but football in general and Newcastle United was one of the big clubs of the time, so I decided to visit St James Park to watch Newcastle play Leeds United, and by the way, the Chief Steward was one of the new crew members to appear. This allowed me to get a "sub " from my wages (£12.00 a month).

The players on view that day included Milburn, Davies and the Robeldo brothers. Schoolar was the team captain. The ground was jam packed shoulder to shoulder. Leeds United had no known " stars" in their team with the exception of one, and what a star he was! John Charles, a Welsh international. He could play in defence or as a centre forward, also known as the gentle giant, a player who never had the need to foul an opponent or show dissent. In this match he lived up to that reputation. Even the Newcastle supporters were in awe of this great player. I was so proud of being a fellow Welshman and also looking forward to telling my dad about the great experience. It was with my dad that I first went to see a big match just after the war sitting on his shoulders at Boothbury Park, Oldham Athletic, watching another great player from my dad's time by the name of George Hardwick.

One morning I was called to the Chief Steward's office to see Mr Smith, He went on to inform me that he had a telegram from my father. He handed it over for me to read, and as it was in Welsh he was unaware of the content. I explained that my grandmother was very ill having suffered a stroke and my father would like me to come home if it was possible.

I had been very apprehensive about Mr Smith as I felt strongly that he had done nothing with regard to my well being and there was a time when I had thought of writing to Port Line and to H.M.S. Conway to highlight my plight, but possibly in hindsight I was glad that I did not. Mr Smith asked if I intended going and that it was up to myself. I had no hesitation in saying yes. He told me to come back in an hour.

It was a long hour to wait, but when I went back he had everything ready for me: a train warrant from Newcastle to Leeds and on to York, Crewe, and Bangor. I was to take with me all my possessions, Port Line would contact me at my home address. I thanked him for his efforts, but as I was about to depart I remembered that I had no money and that I had not had any since joining the ship at King George V docks in London. I would need to pay the Metro from Hebburn to Newcastle and the bus when I reached Caernarfon as well as my regular repast of fish and chips.

To my utter surprise he took out his wallet and gave me £50 in £10 notes. I had never seen a £10 note, let alone been given one. It was a fortune. I thanked him. The Chief Steward, Mr Hetherington, changed one of the £10 notes for 10 single pound notes, it was in those days old currency.

I wasted no time in my departure, but in hindsight should have planned my journey a bit better. Nevertheless, I was soon on the Metro heading for Newcastle station and on to Leeds in no time. A little wait at Leeds and I was on my way to York station but all good things come to an end. No train for Crewe until the morning so I had my fish and chips and slept in the waiting room until the morning. The following morning I was on my way on the very early and slow train to Crewe, and then the Irish Mail from Crewe to Bangor. Not one of the booking offices took the slightest bit of notice of my warrant.

On arriving at Bangor station the man in the booking station recommended that I took a bus to Caernarfon as the next train would be some time in the afternoon so I took a walk to the bus station. My luck was in as a bus was just about to leave. Every bus had a conductor in them days, so I chanced my luck and showed him my train warrant. He smiled and moved on - I was learning fast.

Caernarfon was my home town and in the forties and fifties it was a busy thriving little town. It was where local people met and relations from other areas would converge to pass on news and information. The local paper was The Caernarfon and Denby Herald; another was The Cymro.

The square next to the old castle had pubs and hotels; the war memorial and statues and the old fountain are no longer there. The square was always full of buses starting from the fountain. The Crossville bus to Llanberis passed through my home village of Cwm-Y-Glo; others were Red Star, Blue Star, Whiteways, Clunnog and Trefor; others to Portmadog and other areas, the last in line if I remember correctly was the Bangor bus.

On my arrival I walked across to the queue waiting for the Llanberis bus. There were a lot of faces that I knew, but at the head of the queue was an old friend of my family and a man that I cared about. He looked down the queue and spotted me and came over to greet me.

Idwal Parry was a First world war veteran who had lost a leg in the conflict. He was the village carpenter and undertaker. I had known him throughout my childhood. His first words to me were to offer his condolences with regard to my grandmother. His words hit me hard. I knew at that moment that my grandmother had passed away, but at the back of my mind I did not want to accept it. Idwal realised that I did not know and the pained expression on his face was there to see, fortunately the bus came in and he moved back to the head of the queue.

CHAPTER 10

Last Journey Home.

I sat on the Caernarfon to Llanberis green Crossville bus heading for my home village of Cwm-y-Glo. I somehow knew it would be the last time as such, in future I would be a visitor. My grandmother was the last family connection to the village that had been home to the Jones-Thomas-Roberts family for three hundred years.

Cwm–y-Glo had two bus-stops, one near the school and the other at Craig-y-Don as you leave the village. Should the bus be a bit early it would wait a while at the first stop to make up time.

On the day in question I decided to disembark at the first bus stop: I ran the whole length of the village past the Post Office, Shop Eric and shop Llew Hughes. The old shop at the corner as you turned towards the chapel had not been demolished then, at that point I would have normally come across Mrs Green, but not this time: I entered the back yard via the old gate and opened the back door using the clicker latch, hastened down towards the pantry, turned left half knowing that my grandmother would not be sitting on the settle in the far corner. The back room was exactly the same as usual: on the right the two settles, the table in the middle, the sideboard on the left, the wireless donated by the Blind Association in the corner. The one thing that struck me more than anything was that the fire was out in the grate. I had never seen the room without its coal fire as it would be normal to keep it going all night using wet dross. My grandmother (Nain Cwm) was not there, I somehow knew, but did not want to accept the fact.

I walked through to the front room full of memorabilia. The room had not changed for generations, entered the

83

hall, I thought of going up the stairs but noticed the parlour door was ajar, this would never have been allowed to happen. The parlour was sacrosanct and entry was only allowed by permission, the key was always hidden, but she would allow you in if you asked. I more than anyone else went in to clean and dust as we had a problem with birds falling down the chimney (jackdaws).

I pushed open the door. Her coffin sat across two chairs, my grandmother looked no different, very contented and at peace. I had never seen a dead person but I was not distressed in any way. Some time must have gone by while I stood there until I heard the back door clicker and my dad shouting my name. He was distraught as I knew he would be. He had waited for me at the second bus stop, the one where I would have normally come off the bus and Idwal Parry informed him that I had disembarked at the first.

The few moments my dad and I stood there were very special and will always stay with me. There was the most important member of the family who had seen two world wars, the great flu epidemic, two marriages, the loss of several children through the years, as well as two husbands and her parents, had been part of the lives of her grand children, great and great-great grandchildren, a lady who held an open house for over seventy years. There was no better way for both of us to be part of her passing.

At the time of her death my grandmother was the oldest person living in the village. Well known to everyone, Welsh was her every day language with just a basic knowledge of the English language. She made her mark on her pension book, but otherwise could not read or write. She had lived at Ty Capel (also known as Tan-y-Graig) for over 70 years and paid a rent of 2/6 a year having inherited an agreement from a past owner, a farmer who delivered milk to the village. All the maintenance had to be undertaken by the family.

Ty Capel was an open house with no locks on the doors. The key for the chapel was kept in the hall hanging on an old nail. The chapel key was 10 inches long, a real work of art. Should anyone need to gain entry to the chapel they just helped themself and during my time at Ty Capel the front door would continually open and close as people came in and out.

In my time two of the rooms had electric lights, water was available from a tap near to the back door, the toilet was at the back of the yard. Ty Capel was thought to be updated and one of the better properties in the village at that time.

She had been married twice: first to my blood grandfather Lewis Thomas. He and his family lived next door to the Jones family at New Street, Cwm-y-Glo. My grandmother was 17 years old and Lewis 18 years older. After his death in 1910, she married another village man: an unmarried man and very respected member of the Roberts family, the oldest village family that had moved into the village in the 1700s from the Lleyn peninsula.

My grandmother was very much the matriarch of the family, and dominated the men folk of the household. She did not have the same hold on the female members. My dad in particular was spoiled and pampered being the youngest. When he married my mother, she was aged 19 and he was 35. My grandmother never accepted her and my mother never set foot in Ty Capel. All her children and grandchildren came home in the summer holidays; Azariah and his family from South Wales; Mary from Oldham and the others that lived in local villages would always be in and out. A more comprehensive and detailed history can be found in Chapter 13.

Chapel house (Ty Capel) as I have mentioned was an open house. The milkman, butcher, the cockle and mussels man, the insurance man, the rabbit catcher, all the trade people that visited the village called for a cup of tea. Doctor Douglas was a frequent caller, in fact he had his own cup and would help himself.

This was the reason that she paid only 2/6 a year rent: the then milkman, a farmer always called for a cup of tea and a piece of Bara Brith and left instructions when he passed away that she would live in the house for that nominal sum for the rest of her days.

I was soon to receive a letter from Port Line Ltd with the option of re joining the Port Fremantle or wait for another appointment. I chose to leave the following morning to retrace my journey to Hebburn. When I arrived at Hawthorn Leslie the whole picture had changed. A sense of urgency, cleaning and painting was in progress. My friend John Dixon was directing operations and feeling very important. The new crew including the captain were on board. Sea trials were imminent followed by taking on coal ballast.

CHAPTER 11

Shell Tanker Capsa

Whilst at Hawthorn Leslie, I witnessed the first launching of a big ship, the Shell tanker Capsa. A large crowd had gathered and a spirit of excitement was in the air. She started her journey down the ramps at a snail's pace, but even at that speed when she entered the water the swell and rise of the water level was very exciting. She straddled the river from bank to bank with only what seemed to be inches from the far shore. The noise of the chains and the cheering of the crowd were very loud and all added to the thrill of the moment. All shipping and movement on the river was at a standstill until the tug- boats had turned her round and nudged her to her berth.

Little did I know that my memory of this occasion was to be recalled many years later – not anywhere near the sea, as you would expect, but in the engineering shop at Stewart and Lloyds Ltd, the company I worked with many years later in life.

One of the welder/burners, a chap by the name of Bob Dixon and myself, were having a conversation with regard to working a Sunday shift (overtime). Bob to my surprise had turned down a chance to work, which was unheard of! I ventured to ask his reason for turning down the chance to work a double time Sunday shift. His reply was to my relief not with regard to health or any serious reason, but the fact that his son and family were visiting from Liverpool.

After a while as we chatted he pulled from his wallet a picture of his son, a sea captain and in the background was the Shell tanker Capsa. I was pleased to be able to tell Bob of my part in the vessel's story.

CHAPTER 12

Friday was payday

Friday was payday at Hawthorn Leslie and a mass exodus would converge on the gate at finishing time. The security guard would control the flow of men through the small gate.

Outside the wives and mothers with prams would wait patiently for their husbands, forming a queue up the street. Only a reasonable number exited through the gate at the same time. This was done on purpose to give the womenfolk a chance to grab their men before they made a dash for the nearest pub or the pitch and toss site behind the church. Once in possession of their pay packet a debate would take part, sometimes prolonged and other times the agreement would be long established.

Some of the younger men would attempt to conceal a pound or two in the peak of their caps and other places. They would only get away with it if they had worked over time during that week as the womenfolk knew exactly the amount that should be in the pay packet. Most of the transactions were amicable with just one or two of the men's futile attempts at showing off.

I would stand by the church wall and watch with interest. The smiles and laughter among the women and children were infectious. Now with all the years that have flown by, I realise that all this was part of the tradition and normal way of life at the shipyards in those days. I also realise the part the security men played as by only allowing the men through the small gate a few at a time allowed the women a chance to find their partners.

Not all the workers took part, but what was very noticeable was the fact that the older men were more involved with their grandchildren and also making acquaintance with friends. This was to confirm the importance of this tradition.

CHAPTER 13

Ty Capel (Chapel House in Cwm-y-Glo)

This chapter is about the house and the way of life throughout the time my grandmother lived there as told to me by her, my dad and others, It will give an insight to life through the house and the home that it was.

My grandmother was born Elizabeth Jones, became Thomas by her first marriage and Roberts by her second marriage. She moved to Ty Capel just after her marriage to Lewis Thomas (my grandfather), at the age of seventeen. She lived there over seventy years through the turmoil of two world wars, the great flu epidemic, lost both her husbands there and gave birth to many children; some survived to adulthood and many did not.

The house that is situated near the chapel had many names in its time: Tan–y-Graig, Gladstone House, and Ty Capel. During her time there it was always Ty Capel, it has now reverted to Tan-y-Graig.

In my time there this rambling old house was very basic but having said that, it was most probably recognised as one of the village's better houses. There were just two electric lights: one was in the living room and the other in the back room, the rest of the house was lit by paraffin lamps and candles. The water tap was next to the back door, and the toilet was at the back of the yard in a stone hut built into the corner; it had no door. The back yard was small with a bit of a grass area and a large home made hut in the far corner. Running the length of the house against the back wall, was a slate step that could be used for many things like washing or even sitting down. The hut was used for coal and logs for the fire, other oddments were also stored there.

My time at Ty Capel was only a short window between the late1940s to around 1955. By this time my grandmother was old and suffering with dementia, hence the reason for my sister Betty at first, and then myself being there.

Grandmother rented the house for 2/6 a year, she inherited the agreement from a farmer that delivered milk in the old days. This farmer was one of many who had his tea and possibly his breakfast at Ty Capel. He had left the agreement in his will. It was to remain until she died.

The house had four bedrooms and a very large landing. At the end of the landing there always sat a commode and a basin with two large jugs, or pitchers, on the left side. Hanging from hooks were the towels. The men tended not to use this facility, having a wash and a shave in the back room downstairs. This upstairs facility was vital at night, I suppose.

Downstairs, near to the back door, was a room always referred to as the back room. It was the coldest room in the house as it was intended in the old days to cater for game: rabbits, hares and such. The many shelves had pickle jars, but in my time there was little of the intended material around as my grandmother had become old and things had changed. In olden times game would hang there in abundance: pheasants, rabbits, a hare perhaps. Pickled eggs, onions, red cabbage, herring and many other things would be in bottles on the shelves.

This room was also used as a wash room, mainly for the men and even at my time there the cut-throat razors were still hanging on the nails by the window, one or two safety razors had found their way among them, also the straps that they used for keeping them sharp.

Other oddments like buckets and cleaning tools were also stored here as well as shoes and boots. At the end of the room near the back door that was never locked and only had the clicker to open and close it, were a number of hooks to hang your out-door clothes on. In my time the old clothes that hung there had been there for many years. I often wondered who wore this one and who had worn the other. An umbrella and walking stick stand stood in the corner, never in use in my time.

Down the passage was the pantry built in under the stairs. The pantry held the usual things: Worcester sauce, mustard and always a tin of salmon held for any visitor. Other things like cheese and butter were always covered in a special dish.

Turning left into the back living room, this was the room where my grandmother spent most of her time. It had two settles along one side and an old dresser on the other, down the middle was a long table that was always scrubbed clean and at the end was the large fire place that you could sit inside. The grate was an open fire grate with an oven at the side, two swinging kettle or teapot holders that could be placed over the fire and then retracted when not in use. At either side of the fireplace were the coal buckets: one to hold prime coal and logs, the other for dross, and the other usual things like the all important poker, a brush and other odds and ends. Above this area was a line that was used for hanging out wet towels, and the fender.

The long table that took most of the space down the middle of the room had the salt pot, pepper and a bottle of Camp coffee, horrible stuff that nobody liked. Also on the table permanently was the Aladdin lamp and a smaller paraffin lamp. The Aladdin lamp gave a good light, white and clear, but was difficult to light and I never did master it. The other lamp was the stand by. This one gave a poor light more red and dull, it was also dirty and the fumes and smoke were not very healthy. The glass had to be cleaned every other day.

The salt pot was an open pot that you would take a pinch of salt out of, not the fine salt that you get today. My grandmother would buy a block of salt that would last for ever, it seemed.

On the floor were two small carpets or rugs, home made with rags and very heavy. They would get very dirty and would need shaking outside every morning.

On the other side of the room running along under the window that overlooked the back yard, was an old dresser without its top. Very heavy and it was a permanent fixture as nobody in their right mind would attempt to move it. The fixtures on the top never changed. Whenever a newspaper was bought it would be added to a heap in the corner after being read, they would be later used for lining drawers and for toilet paper. Letters, bills, reminders, pools coupons, pens and pencils and everyday items were always there. In the other far corner was the most prized possession: a radio that had a brass label saying it was "donated by the blind association" on the front. It was large with a number of valves that would have to be replaced now and again, but could pick up the world championship boxing from America as well as local stations.

The radio brings back memories of my dad and his brothers listening to the boxing. I would go to bed early and then get up in the middle of the night to listen to Tommy Farr the Welsh heavy-weight, fighting the great American heavyweight champion Joe Lewis. Other boxers were Jimmy Wilde, Jim Driscole, and may others. Boxing was a big sport among the Welsh miners and quarrymen.

The one story that I must include derives from my grandmother's love of cats: ginger tom cats in particular, and there would always be one in the living room during day time; at night he would get thrown out to fend for himself. Their life span was short as in those days they were never neutered and their wanderings after females took its toll.

I remember the one that was there during my time. He would sit next to my grandmother on the narrow arm of the old settle and move with her swaying movement. My grandmother in old age would sway side-wards to the left and then to the right alternating by moving backwards and forward. The cat would sway with her to perfection never miss-timing the sway on a very narrow settle arm. My grandmother would get fed up with him and from time to time she would sweep him off the settle arm, but he would be back in no time.

She also had a good head of hair and I mention this as it was a wonder that she had any hair at all. Hanging from a shelf inside the fire place was a pair of hair tongs very similar to a pair of scissors with one blade a solid tube and the other a half round blade that would accept the round tube after it had been heated in the fire. She would heat it up and then dip it in cold water, then when the temperature was right she would curl her hair. It would sizzle and smell, but certainly curled her hair.

The back room was dark and in evening time it would throw shadows that scared me as a child.

Moving out of the back living room past the pantry you came upon the main living room and the largest room in the house. This room was always clean with proper bought carpets on the floor. On your right was a long sideboard with many cupboards full of linen towels and such like. On the top stood two porcelain lions with orange manes and white bodies, each at either end of the cupboard top. In the middle stood many vases, jugs, teapots and glassware. The wall above had the usual pictures and plates hanging on the wall.

At the far end as you turned the corner was a wall cupboard that stood from floor to the ceiling. In the middle was the fireplace and at the other end the wall cupboard was exactly the same as the one at the other end. They held all kind of things: crockery, tea set's plates and all kind of other things.

The fireplace that was out of this world with old tiles around it, the fire place was black-leaded until it gleamed. All kind of brass objects stood inside the fender along with the poker, shovel and brush. Along the top above the fireplace was a shelf that had German shell casings from the first war all engraved with dragons and unicorns and such like. They were all brass and would need polishing from time to time. My uncle Owen (Now Bach) who was my grandmother's second oldest son, had brought them back from the first world war. He was born in 1900 and enrolled late in the conflict. He served for a time after the war in clearing up operations with his regiment The Royal Engineers.

The wall running along the front had a large window that was heavily curtained. In front was a couch with two reclining chairs, a polished table and four chairs. In the corner was another fitted cupboard similar to the other two on the fire place wall. Next was the door that led into the hall. This door was again something special: leaded glass of many colours.

Along the fourth wall was a glass cupboard or you could call it a display cabinet. The top and bottom were full of memorabilia items that sons and daughters and indeed friends had brought back from past holidays or visits to other climes, items marked "Welcome to Llandudno" and many other destinations, small vases, dog and cat figurines (many ginger cats). My grandmother also kept her paper money in one special jug; it was meant to be a secret but everyone knew about it.

Through the glass door to the large hall that was wood panelled, dark and well used. On the right were the coat hooks with coats and jackets from generations back hanging there, lifeless. Umbrellas and walking sticks were in one corner, in the other corner hanging on a nail was the chapel key along with the gate key. The key was massive and would be hard for anyone to misplace. People would enter the front door regularly for the key to gain entrance to the chapel. The front door was never locked, in fact it never even had a lock.

The other wall only had the door to the parlour that was always kept locked, the key kept in a safe place and like many Welsh abodes the parlour was a special room that kept family heirlooms and pictures / photographs and personal items, but its main purpose was a rather more gloomy aspect. When a death occurred in the family, the dead person would lay in his/her coffin between two chairs until the day of the funeral which was usually a Saturday. My grandmother had many such occasions in her lifetime: her father, two husbands and many children. It was also there, the last time I was to set eyes on my beloved grandmother standing over her coffin with my father.

I was permitted to gain entry now and again because of birds falling down the chimney, jackdaws in particular. They would make an almighty mess and getting them outside was an arduous task.

This brings me to another story that made me very unpopular in the village. I decided to keep one jackdaw chick in a cardboard box and did manage to bring him up as a pet. He regarded me as his mother and the cardboard box had to be up-graded to something like a hen hut for my noisy pet. Not only did he become a nuisance and a scourge to the old and young in the village by landing on someone's head without any warning, he would follow me everywhere and I would have to lock him up while I went to school. Even this caused a problem in that all his friends, brothers and sisters, and all the jackdaws in the community, would attempt to free him.

The problem had to be solved by my poor dad. Not the best cyclist in the world, he had to borrow a bike and one Sunday afternoon we cycled as far as possible to release our friend to the wild. Followed by the jackdaw's supporters club, we set out very early before the villagers found out our intentions and cycled as far as we could. When the supporters club had diminished to zero we decided that it would be safe to rid ourselves of the pest, we gave him a good meal and said our goodbye. Luck was on our side as it was the last we saw of him. The local community was delighted.

The stairs led upwards from the hall into a very large landing: two bed rooms in the back and two in the front. At the front between the two bedrooms on the landing was an area designated for the ladies of the house to "toilet": a commode with washing utensils, two large water jugs and a towel rack.

All the bedrooms were of the same size; the two back rooms were for visitors and would only be used in the summer. My grandmother's had been adjusted to accommodate her old age. The bed had been lowered and another commode placed in the room itself. My grandmother only removed her outer clothes at bedtime. Her two daughters, my Auntie Nell and Auntie Sydney, would strip wash and make her presentable every Friday. All this may seem odd and very different to life today, but it must be remembered that the area where we lived in North Wales was way behind the rest of the country. There were no residential care or homes, no sheltered accommodation, the family did the caring the best way they could. Hot water had to be boiled in the yard; the house was cold in the winter; limited electric light. The two sisters had their work cut out and it took time.

Well there you are - Ty Capel (Chapel House). If only the old house could have told its own story.

Ty Capel : My grandmother's home for over seventy years is now known as Tan-y-Graig. The chapel is clearly shown on the right of this picture. Mr and Mrs Green lived in the house next door. "Gromlech " is to the right of the chapel, Mrs Beatrice Hughes, a brave and wonderful lady, lived in the first house, and during my childhood Melvin and Selwyn Pritchard, brothers and school friends, lived there. Melvin was a great football player - the David Beckham of the village. Melvin and Selwyn, like myself, were the two rascals.

The Jones side of my family settled in "Gromlech" at around 1800 before moving to New Street.

CHAPTER 14

M.V. Port Fremantle - Continued.

My stay at home was very short and I was soon on my way back to Hebburn to rejoin the M.V. Port Fremantle. I did however receive a letter from Port Line offering me the choice of going back or wait for another appointment.

The journey back was very much the same with the exception of the sleepless night in the station waiting room. Again, neither the station booking office or anyone else took notice of my travel warrant.

On my arrival at Hawthorn Leslie I found the whole situation had changed. John Dixon was as efficient as ever. He stood at the top of the gangway checking all the movement in and out of the vessel. He soon directed me to the same cabin that I was again to share with my friend Thompson. John was full of authority and gave me my instructions, showed me round the ship. The forecastle and the engine-room were out of bounds as far as I was concerned. I was to be on the captain's watch, and was reminded never to be late on watch.

The ship was due to undertake sea-trials followed by a visit to Blyth to take on ballast then the voyage would start by facing the north Atlantic ocean.

Before that I should mention my "sea sickness" and the fact that I have never throughout my life managed to get on top of it. It would start the moment the ship was under way and continue for two days. The weather or the conditions made no difference, I would be so bad that I could do absolutely nothing and the weight loss was dramatic, however, when I did emerge I would have no further problems until the ship reached port - only to be the same again when the ship was again under way.   To underline the problem I will mention a story that happened on my honeymoon, years after I had left the Merchant Navy.

On our honeymoon, we decided to take a short trip on a motor launch from the harbour at Paignton in Devon to the harbour at Brixham, a trip on no distance whatsoever. We settled on a bench facing forward directly in front of a bar and atop the bar was a beer pump depicting a Red Barrel. One look at the Red Barrel going up and down against the background porthole was all that was required!

I dreaded the sea sickness, but had to put it aside and get on with it. On the whole I settled down and enjoyed the experience and I soon became very popular with the officers and all the crew that I came across. The captain was a Welshman like myself and we became very good friends. He was from Flintshire and spoke Welsh when we were alone. The memory of Captain Conby has stayed with me all my life. Another person who made a big impression on me was the quartermaster, a Scot from Inverness called Mac Macdonald. He was Gaelic spoken and would take great interest in my letters from home that my dad always wrote in Welsh.

The highlight of my watch was when the quartermaster allowed me to take the wheel whilst he went for a toilet break or to drink his tea. The officers would sometimes let me work out the course and I seldom got it wrong. I had taken a great interest in the slide rule at H.M.S. Conway and felt confident with that kind of exercise.

However, I had no real work to do, Running to and from the galley with the mugs of chocolate/ tea/ coffee/ soup was to be my main task. The ship had a radar that was newly fitted and everyone took a great interest in it. The radio was situated at the rear of the ship in a special cabin on the poop deck, Mr T Cartwright was the wireless operator, he would appear on the bridge from time to time, but I did not get to know him very well, however he was to become known to all before the end of this voyage. (I will come to that later.)

John Dixon was the senior cadet / seventh officer and I was the junior cadet. On the previous trip Thompson was the junior, on this trip he had progressed to the engine room as a first year apprentice. With a bit of luck I would follow that route. I was known as Junior and John Dixon loved to use that term whenever he was about. Others had the usual names: the first officer was The Mate, second officer was Second and so on down to the seventh officer; then we had the sparkies - the electrical engineers; the engineers were Chief, First / Second and so on. There were others like the Bosun, carpenter (Chippy), and Donkey–man who ran the engines, the chief cook, the second cook and the baker; the Chief Steward/Purser and his staff. They were known by what they did rather than by name.

The galley was admidships – it ran across left to right, port side to the starboard side, the bakery was at one end, the cooking range running the whole length. All the cooking utensils hung on chains to allow for the rolling movement of the vessel. One big urn-like pot sat in the middle containing the stock for the soup, this was kept continually on the boil. Puree was added depending on the flavour that was required on the day. I was well-in with the old chief-cook and could help myself to a mug of soup any time, and also a bacon or egg sandwich and there were times when I needed the nourishment following a bout of sea sickness.

The Chief Steward / Purser, a chap called Hethrington, also became a friend and I would occasionally assist him with his book keeping and office work. There were not the computers and calculators that we have today, just pen and paper and ledger that had to be kept up to date.

The first voyage and my first time at sea were very exciting, I remember every port of call, but not in the right order - like the first names of a lot of the crew, the memory has let me down a bit.

We arrived at Kingston, Jamaica on a bright and clear morning. Later in the afternoon it was to become very hot. You could put out a tin plate with a bit of butter on it and fry an egg by just the heat off the sun. While we waited out in the bay for a berth, the local women would row their boats out to pick up our laundry. We would lower our pillowcase filled up with our soiled laundry, and include our name, then lower it to the waiting lady in the boat. The following morning it would be returned all clean. They charged next to nothing. We could pay in American dollars or Pound sterling.

Other boats would have provisions, and others bananas that were sold very green still on the branch, far too many really and when they became ripe they all came at once. First time visitors like myself gorged ourselves.

The captain had given me very firm instructions as regard going ashore, but I foolishly ignored his advice and was talked into going with two of the seamen "Blonde" and "Paddy". It was a lesson learned and I was not inclined to go again.

The story was something like this: Blonde and Paddy asked me if I would like to go ashore with them, they were to meet other members of the crew at a bar not far from the dock area. We arrived at the bar, an open area similar to a pub garden in the UK. It was well populated with a lot of girls and seamen of many nationalities. Blonde bought a bottle of rum that cost next to nothing. The coke was another thing, it cost an arm and a leg, and a lot of bartering went on. After a while, my two companions disappeared and I was left on my own. By this time I had regrets and felt vulnerable and it did not take long for me to decide to depart. I left as quietly as possible, and made my way back to the ship. This was not easy as I had not taken a lot of notice of my route. It was a bit like when you park your car at the airport and have not noted the details.

I arrived at the dock gate, a red funnel stood behind the cargo shed. I made my way to the ship and up the gangway only to be approached by a Japanese officer, I was on the wrong ship and totally confused. I searched the area to no avail and decided to seek the advice of the dock security man at the gate, but when I arrived at the gate I realised that I was at the wrong area, I should have gone to the next gate, To my great relief I found the ship. I made nothing of my adventure to the officer on the gangway and made my way to my cabin and then walked on to the galley to see my friend the chief cook. He made me some supper and he was the only person I confided in.

I felt that I had let the captain and others down, I had not used any common sense. I went ashore a lot in the weeks and months that followed with no apprehension, I had I think learned a lesson.

The next port of call was Port-of-Spain in Trinidad: I did take some shore leave and found the people very friendly, cricket was the main topic on the island and the lunch-time games on the make shift pitch behind the cargo sheds was taken very seriously. I took part in one of these games and scored a very creditable two runs, both leg-bye's but nevertheless two runs. I was out with the next ball, my wicket sent flying back to Jamaica.

All the players had the same names "Gary Sobers " and

took the games very seriously, I could not take a chance in playing any more for the fear of injury: they also used a hard rubber ball.

The following Saturday or Sunday we had to participate in a proper game; a lot more sedate and less competitive. We had to wear whites and all the ship's officers made up the team. My part in all this was to take on to the field of play a tray of drinks now and again. I was not considered for a place in the team, and I cannot remember if we won or not or who we played.

The next island we visited was Curacao also in the Caribbean. The purpose of the visit was to re-fuel. We tied up at a long jetty and although no shore leave was allowed one or two of us decided to walk along to the shore end, The jetty was narrow with the fuel pipe running its length.

As we progressed along the jetty we notice the frenzy of activity both in the sea and in the sky. The sea birds were going mad, and when we came closer to the shore we noticed the reason why: the whole area adjacent to the jetty and along the shore line was covered with small lizards, so dense that you had to walk on them. If you stood still they would walk up your legs. Rocks, walls and buildings were totally covered. The birds were gorging themselves and the fish under the jetty like wise. We had to go back very smartly to avoid being covered. I had never seen any thing like it.

We were soon on our way again; several visits in South America, San Francisco, where I did see the Golden Gates, but not a lot more, and finally to New York. The New York skyline was very spectacular but strangely it was for something else that I remember New York.

The crew had to line up on deck to wait for a visit by an immigration officer: a lady immigration officer. She gave us a short-arm inspection as well as checking our teeth and hair, finishing off with a lecture on behaviour while visiting the city. We had two or three D.P. 's (displaced persons) among the crew: they were not allowed ashore. The stay was not long and our next destination was Canada, St Johns Nova Scotia, and with the winter setting in I was in for a shock.

We arrived at St Johns on a bitterly cold morning in December. Snow and ice were setting in and the locals were busy getting the ice rinks that seem to be on every street corner ready for the seasonal activities. A new film star sensation was showing at the cinema: James Dean in a film called Giant.

I was not ready for the cold weather and had to buy some clothes: warm shoes and a proper hat was very necessary. You had to make sure your nose, mouth and ears were well protected. A good scarf was also important, It took me a few days to get accustomed to it. We did not stay long at St Johns and moved on to Halifax and our stay there was possibly the longest of the whole trip.

We again arrived in the morning and waited a while for a berth. The area around the harbour was frozen and within a few days the whole harbour was iced up. Ice breakers (a trawler like ship with a strong bow) were used to keep the harbour from freezing solid.

Life on a tramping vessel in extreme weather is not very pleasant. I was never warm the whole of the time that I was there. The toilet become frozen, no running water, your clothes seemed to be damp all the time and you dared not step outside without protecting your face, hands and other parts.

I did go out a lot and enjoyed the town and its people. Ice hockey and skating were played at most street corners, but I never did get the hang of it.

The next destination was Brisbane, Australia via the Panama canal, but that was a long way off. The loading of the vessel was slow work owing to the weather and Christmas was only a few days away. The cargo was again general cargo, but the main bulk was paper reams destined for the news paper industry. They were massive things and each must have weighed a considerable amount. They took two cranes to load them and they were delivered to the docks on low-loaders and with the icy roads deliveries were slow.

Christmas was on us, but our existence on board was grim; everything was frozen and the cold was overbearing, but the sun shines on the righteous and I was to get a surprise that I will never forget.

CHAPTER 15

Halifax, Nova Scotia.

The day before Christmas I was called in to see the captain, I was a bit apprehensive wondering if I had done something wrong, but I need not have worried. Captain Conby informed me that he had arranged for me to spend the Christmas Day and the Boxing Day with friends of his. I was to get myself ready, dress in my uniform and take an overnight bag. I was to behave and not to let him down. To be honest I was very unsure as to what was ahead of me.

A big American type car pulled up on the wharf. I was invited to sit in the front seat alongside the driver. I was to find out a bit later that he was the head of the household and could not have been more friendly and welcoming. The car had some kind of "straps" over the back wheels to give the car traction on the icy roads.

We arrived at a large house on the outskirts of the town. Christmas lights covered the front of the house and were all along the drive. I was invited in and met the family, the lady of the house and a boy who was possibly a bit younger than I, and a girl who was older. I had my own room and they made me very welcome. As the day went on, more people arrived and this made it a lot easier for me. Time went on and Christmas Eve was party time. They played games and played Christmas music and insisted that I was involved.

Christmas Day was out of this world. I had never experienced anything like it. The amount of food and drink was something I had never been accustomed to. At home we had the basic, Dad would have bred a cockerel in the back garden especially for Christmas, gifts or presents were unheard of.

After dinner, the family and all the guests sang carols and the father dressed up as Father Christmas to distribute gifts to everyone. I felt embarrassed but made an attempt not to show it. When it was my turn to receive a gift, I was overwhelmed, I was given a Lumberjack Shirt that I had for many years after. Even my sister Betty took a fancy to the shirt; I noticed that it kept going missing from my drawer at home now and again. I will never forget the kindness of the family. I was accepted into the family at the most important time for any family, and to Captain Conby for giving me the opportunity. I was taken back to the ship, I made several attempts to find out who the family was so I could write to thank them, but Captain Conby would not even mention the event.

The weather had got worst. The cold was so intense that the harbour froze solid with no movement of shipping. The loading of our vessel was slow. This I found was hard on all concerned. A lot of the seamen drank too much. The time on their hands was not advantageous to them or to anyone else, painting was out of the question as the ship was covered in ice.

The time to depart came at last. The holds were full and well covered and all hands was busy getting the ship ready. With great excitement I noticed the "Blue Peter" aloft and activities in the harbour had increased, I also noticed that most of the ships that had been there as long as us were going as well.

Explosives were used to initially break the ice. Several thuds were heard followed by the ice breakers preparing a path for the vessels to make their way through. Once out in the bay the ships were able to get under way. The fun and games were to come later when we moved to warmer climates. While in Halifax, we used the toilets on the wharf as the ship's were frozen solid. The same for washing and no one seemed to shave: clothes were being laundered at the minimum, I for one was glad to be on our way. After a day or two I noticed the ship's carpenter was very busy getting buckets and all kind of things ready for something. Little did I know what was coming.

Pipes started to defrost and the toilet pans developed cracks. All hands were busy with mops and buckets. The carpenter was working flat out. After a while some sort of order was regained. All this to me was something new, but I suppose they took it all in their stride.

We left Halifax outward bound for the Panama Canal. Through the canal and then to the Pacific Ocean to Brisbane in Australia. I was to go through my usual bout of seasickness and missed the cleaning up operation that had to be undertaken when we reached warmer waters.

Otherwise, the trip to the Panama was uneventful. The great thrill of the Panama Canal was a wonderful experience: at the Atlantic side we picked a pilot and a crew that would be in charge of our progress through. The pilot and Captain Conby spent a lot of their time in debate while the crew and ship's crew enjoyed some magic moments. They had guitars and entertained us all as we sailed through the most tropical part of the world. Birds such as parrots flew overhead and sometimes landed on the ship. The colours were breath taking.

Captain Conby must have relaxed the no alcohol rule on board ship and while we sailed through the Canal beer was allowed.

The ship entered a series of locks that were then flooded and a powerful tractor was used to pull the vessel to the next lock. They called them 'mules'. Another vessel worked the locks on the way down in exactly the same way. I found it all very exciting.

Leaving the locks behind us we travelled through some lakes with forest and jungle on each side of us. The traffic was heavy with vessels following in line with a reasonable distance between them. We finally arrived at the Pacific and a place they called Colon, if I remember correctly. The same procedure to lower the vessel through the locks and then it was goodbye to the pilot and his crew. We anchored out in the bay, making preparations for our long trip across the Pacific.

After my usual two days recovery time from yet another bout of sea sickness, I began to enjoy the calm sea and tropical weather. The sea was like a mirror with only the path of the vessel following behind. Evening was also exhilarating, every star seemed to be bigger and more sparkling than I was accustomed to.

The Captain allowed sunbathing on the ship's deck as we had no passengers. We watched films on deck in the evening. I remember two of the films very well: The Caine Mutiny with Humphrey Bogart and other great actors of the time; the other was The Sea Chase. I took the opportunity to visit every nook and cranny on board the ship and made the acquaintance of other crew members. I visited the engine room and with my cabin mate, Thompson, enjoyed the atmosphere in the relatively calm period. The noise of the great pistons was subdued and we could hear each other talk.

But as the old saying goes: All good things come to an end. Little did I know that we were in the cyclone season in the Pacific and Cyclone Clara was about to make our acquaintance.

CHAPTER 16

Cyclone Clara.

Good weather had become the normal, but we were about to be tested. A slight change in the sea, the ocean developed a swell - only slight to start with then increasing to make the ship pitch. The blue cloudless sky was still there and the temperature was hot and clammy.

During the night a complete change had occurred and the morning was wet with heavy rain and a rough sea was running. The ship was pitching and rolling. This was to continue throughout the day and it was not until the following day that Captain Conby and his officers showed real concern.

The storm was upon us with the ferocity that cyclones can become. The rain came down in sheets. The wind was also gusting, but the main problem was the sea - large swells and deep troughs, the ship was pitching and rolling like mad, throwing everything about and almost impossible to keep your feet.

My cabin was mid-ship, above the engine room with the galley between my cabin and the bridge superstructure making the crossing near the number two hatch very hazardous indeed, in fact: dangerous. As the captain had instructed the crew to batten down the hatches (as the saying goes), safety ropes were used to cross any open area. A rope was tied at both ends with rings connected to the main rope. You would clip yourself to the ring, then another rope would be tied around your waist and held by a person at the end that you were headed for. This would allow that person to pull you in should you lose your footing or be hit by a wave. This was very necessary. The only problem with it, you would be soaking wet when you reached the other end and being in wet clothes was not very pleasant for the next four hours.

The bulk- heads were dripping wet with condensation, with wet damp beds to put up with. Mealtimes was also a big problem. The cook did his best but warm food and drink was impossible for him to provide.

On the bridge the Captain and his senior officers had to make a decision, and the way I understood the problem was as follows: the ship was heading straight and on course for the eye of the storm and the safest course was head on, meeting the swells and troughs going forward. Turning the ship around was a major hazard as the most vulnerable position, and broad side to the storm, would make it almost impossible for the vessel to cope. During all the pitching and rolling, the radio aerial had been knocked out so we had been unable to make contact with shore to let anyone know what we were doing.

113

But, at the end of the day, it was the only way out as the ship was shipping water and being heavy with a full cargo she was deep in the water and taking longer and longer to recover. We seemed to take ages to come up from each pitch and the noise was horrific. We began our very slow turn late morning. The operation to turn the vessel so that she had her back to the storm was a slow process making a long circle. We took a terrific pounding, but the old girl eventually made it. The relief was noticeable as we raced back the way we came.

Mr Cartwright, the radio engineer, was now able to work on his portable transmitter and after a while was able to make contact with the Australian coastguard. After a day or two we noticed a sea-plane above and eventually a destroyer from the Australian navy paid us a visit.

Having turned our back on the storm, we had gone well back on our course and had to set out a new course for Brisbane, but the next few days were without any incidents. The crew were busy cleaning up and eating normal food at last.

Our arrival at Brisbane was something we will never forget. The press were there in numbers and as the youngest member of the crew, they made a lot of fuss over me. Our wireless operator, Mr T Cartwright, was interviewed and had his name and picture in the papers, also Captain Conby was interviewed several times. The ship was in a mess covered in streaks of rust that took several days to paint out. My Mam was at last informed by Port Line that I was safe and well. It was a worrying time for the family as it had been announced on the news that our ship was missing in the cyclone. To add to their apprehension, they had only just moved to Corby and settling down was not easy.

The Port Fremantle berthed in the Brisbane river having arrived from Panama two days overdue. She had been missing in the Pacific since February 9th, when at long last Mr Cartwright managed to make radio contact. Captain Conby was to report in the newspaper that it was the closest he had ever been to the eye of a cyclone and that he had been a worried man. We were the centre of attention for a few days, but it was soon all over and we returned to normality.

The ship was cleaned up and the rust steaks painted out and after partial off loading we prepared to sail around the coast visiting Sydney, Melbourne, Geelong, Perth and Adelaide, off loading in each port as we went along. I enjoyed my visit to Sydney and walked across the harbour bridge the old way before they made the adjustment for the tourist trade, also visited an amusement park near to the bridge. The Sydney zoo was a special visit, I had wanted to see the Australian wild dog the Dingo as they called it. The zoo was as good a zoo as I have seen.

Bondi Beach was another eye opener with the net buried in the sand to keep the sharks out. The Olympic Games were being held at Melbourne and although I did not see any of the events there was great excitement and the Australians were so keen to do well. I cannot remember a lot about Geelong except that near to the docks there was an army ordnance depot that had everything from tanks to water carriers. Adelaide was very nice, possibly my favourite place in Australia. Perth was very hot, the road from the docks was long and all along its length were orchards with apples, pears and all kind of fruit. You could pick one and it was sweet and ripe.

The Australians like to give you the impression that they are macho men and I remember going into a dock-side pub (I should not be allowed as you had to be twenty one years of age and I was still only 17). It was really a dive with prostitutes at work and along the bottom of the counter, a spittoon for the drinkers to spit in while at the bar. And no, I did not participate.

My grandson Casey's mum now lives at Perth, and tells me how it has changed, and is a great city to live in. As we travelled around the coast we could see the smoke from the bush fires, a common occurrence in Australia. Having discharged most of our cargo we headed for New Zealand.

Ship missing; search order

A widespread search of the south-west Pacific has been ordered for the 8,553-ton British motorship Port Fremantle, now two days overdue in Brisbane.

The passenger and cargo ship left St. John (Canada) on January 5 and was due to sail direct from Panama to Brisbane.

No radio communication has been received from the ship since February 9, when it was 1,200 miles east of Norfolk Island, which is about 975 miles east of Brisbane.

All Australian and New Zealand ships operating in the area have been alerted to watch for the Port Fremantle and the RAAF has been asked to make a search.

The Sydney director of Port Line Ltd. (Mr. D. G. Holebone) has confirmed the vessel is missing.

Port Fremantle should have confirmed on or about February 13 for expected arrival date in Brisbane, he said.

"No information has been received, nor have any shore stations been able to contact the vessel.

"The Navigation Department has been requested to institute immediate emergency steps," said Mr. Holebone.

Radio silence

Fears are held because of the absence of radio messages.

Shipping officials claim that the ship could have foundered or suffered damage to its radio in the big seas whipped up by the cyclone that has been wandering about 300 miles off the Queensland coast for the past fortnight.

It is not known in Brisbane what passengers or cargo were on board the Port Fremantle when it left Panama.

117

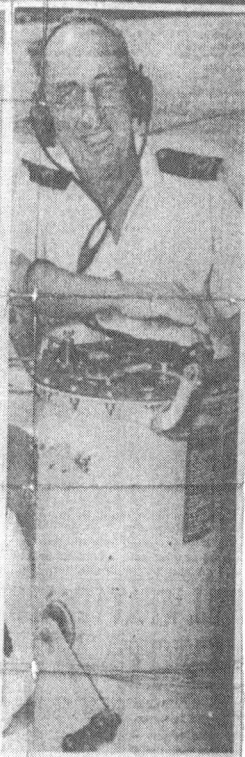

RADIOED 'SAFE AT SEA'

RUST-STREAKED hull of the British freighter Port Fremantle as the vessel swung into its berth yesterday.

Ship's battle with cyclone

"WE were rolling heavily and shipping water . . . parts of the ship were flooded . . . torrential rain was coming down in sheets . . . I was very worried."

Out of touch

A widespread search which was called off for the ship in which Captain Conby sailed off a few weeks ago. . . .

Captain Conby said yesterday that in five days after . . . the ship . . .

When officials of the . . . were told last . . . Sunday when . . . 600 miles . . . Brisbane . . .

Captain H. R. Conby, master of the 8583-ton British freighter Port Fremantle, said this yesterday.

He was expecting . . .

The Port Fremantle berthed in the Brisbane River from Panama yesterday, almost two days overdue.

She had been "missing" in the South-west Pacific since February 6, when she last made radio contact with land.

"Very worried"

. . . Capt. Conby

EMERGENCY wireless transmitter from a lifeboat which was used by Wireless Officer E. Cartwright of the Port Fremantle to report the vessel's position.

CHAPTER 17

New Zealand

Having enjoyed Australia, I would have considered moving there at some point, the only thing that was very apparent was the plight of the aboriginal people. Things have improved they tell me, but in the 1950s and 60s they were a major problem to an otherwise great country. The availability of cheap wine being the big problem, the older people unable to deal with it and the younger ones not having work or wanting to work, abused themselves with the wine that was known as "plonk". This was poison and should have been used to clear the drains.

New Zealand was a beautiful island, in fact two islands, the north and the south islands separated by the Cook Strait. I did not realise this until I arrived there, so much for my geography!

The people seem to get on very well and made us very welcome. I visited the two major cities of Auckland and Wellington, but spent the rest of the time at a small town called Timaru on the Canterbury plains of South Island. The ship needed to be cleaned and prepared for taking on a new cargo of frozen lamb for the European market. The Port Fremantle was a refrigerated vessel that was purpose built for the Canterbury lamb trade. It was vital that the work was carried out as a failure in the refrigeration would have been a catastrophe. This was to take some time, but at least it gave me and one or two others a chance to settle to a routine.

The loading took some time as the frozen lamb was transported from sheep stations along the coast. These stations were said to have slaughter houses and refrigerated plants and housed hundreds of sheep. Rumours said that the population of the country was less than the sheep population by half. Never the less I was pleased that it was taking time as I had found my first girl friend, a girl called Dawn. I did visit Dawn's home. Her Mum, Dad and brother lived in a bungalow high and overlooking the town. From their living room you could see a mountain range and standing high and snow capped was Mount Cook, New Zealand's highest mountain. Dawn's brother was a well known rugby player and at the time was recovering from a broken leg.

The music at the coffee bar was pre-rock and roll, Bill Halley and the Comets had not arrived there at that time. If I remember, Guy Mitchell was singing the blues, but we all enjoyed it just the same. I wrote to Dawn for some time after I got home with good intentions, but other things got in the way and eventually we lost contact. When the time came to sail I was saddened but had to get on with it, possibly a good learning curve.

The trip home went very well. I was given a lot more work to do and the time went by very quickly. We eventually arrived at Avonmouth, Bristol, said our good byes and were paid off. All this was very normal for most of the crew, but for me, being the first time, it was a bit upsetting. My £12.00 a month wages did not get me very far. This time I had to pay my train fare home and by the time I arrived home I was penniless.

Now that nearly 60 years have gone by and a lot has happen in my life I wonder and think back: how did Thompson get on, did he stay at sea, did he ever get married? As far as John Dixon is concerned I imagine he did stay at sea and possibly became a captain, he was very much that type of a guy. Many of the others will have all gone by now, that's for sure.

I never went back to sea, but I will cover that part of my life in the next chapter.

CHAPTER 18

The Move to Corby

I paid off at the port of Avonmouth and travelled to Bristol for the train to Kettering in Northamptonshire. I had never been to that area before and it seemed a long journey. At Kettering station I travelled by bus via the villages of Geddington and Stanion. The last part of the journey was to take me through Stanion Lane towards Corby Old Village and finally Corby Town centre.

Dad moved to Corby first, followed by the family in December 1956. A lot had happened in that year: my mother had been reconciled with her own mother only for her to pass away a few weeks after; my grandmother Nain Cwm had also died; I had left H.M.S. Conway to join Port Line Ltd and was at dry-dock in Hebburn-on-Tyne.

Dad was to be employed by S&L that was at the time opening a new plant within its complex called the Plug-Mill Department and with a background in engineering he was deemed suitable for that kind of work. That was where he was employed until his retirement at 65 years old.

He was to stay at Brigstock-camp initially and then Weldon camp, both close to Corby. He had fellow workers from the quarry there as well. Will Rowland and his wife and two children from Cwm-y-Glo; Will Penny and several more from Llanberis; Bob Griffiths and his family from Waenfawr.

Some years later, Will Rowland and his family were to move and settle in Australia. He was well known and well liked in Corby because of his old Welsh habit of acknowledging all and sundry with a nod of the head and saying "sid-mai". He was to be known as "Noddy".

Dafydd Munro was another who was as Welsh as the hills but carried his father's name and I think he was a Londoner. They called Dafydd "the Cockney Welshman" in the E.R.W. Plant where he worked. I would make a point of meeting up with Dafydd as I could always have a conversation in my beloved Welsh language with Dafydd.

Tom Owen (in Welsh Twm Fawr) was another person who was well known around town. There were many more but they have now all gone, like most of my own family and having a conversation in Welsh is now virtually impossible.

I had lost touch with John "Kate" Thomas many years back and was by now well into my retirement but still following my life long pastime of running when I was approached by a very tall young man who confronted me at a race, stating that his father knew me. I asked him his father's name and when he said John Thomas and that he lived in the town of Rugby I was totally confused. I asked him to give me a bit of time to think about it but unfortunately after the race he had disappeared.

After some consideration I did manage to work it out and made arrangements to meet John at another running race this time at Rugby. I waited at a given spot and the only person in the right age group was not my childhood image of John. My wife Margaret insisted that it must be him after all I had not seen John for 55 years so I went over to him. He spoke Welsh from the start as if we had never been away. We re-established a very rewarding friendship that went on for another five years until his passing two years ago. We went over old ground visiting Llew Hughes, Mair in bwlch, Maldwyn Leslie and Mari Wyn. John Kate never lost his roots and I can only thank his son Peter for getting the two John Thomas's together again.

I will never forget the autumn colours of the trees along Stanion Lane on that first journey to Corby. My two youngest sisters, Eluned and Sandra, met me off the bus and we walked the short distance to Leighton Road where my family lived. Mam was adamant that I was not to go back to sea and as there was plenty of work in the town I was soon to be employed at S&L tube-works in the town.

She had despatched my father to see the labour relations officer even before I had arrived home, I was to complete 43 years service there and was Chief Inspector for Corby West Works when I retired. My family had settled reasonably well and my sisters had all found their feet at school, and with both my mother and father working the family had prospered.

We soon moved from Leighton Road to Weldon where my mother bought a house, but unfortunately not before a lot of heartache and ups and downs. Mam and Dad were having problems, it had been noticeable for some time. Dad was getting old and as my mother was a lot younger it was a problem. Life in Corby was a lot different to North Wales. The prosperity and new ways of life were so different and they struggled to readjust.

My sisters suffered the most. My eldest sister in particular, Betty Wyn was the most beautiful girl and hence attracted a lot of attention. Adolescence was hard for her and eventually problems came her way. She married young, lost her little boy in a road accident and had to give up her new born daughter to adoption, and with her marriage in ruins she had to start life all over again.

Her second marriage to Robert Herhold, an American, made up for the first. They had two wonderful children and as a family they prospered. She was also able to have contact with her adopted daughter before Betty passed away in her fifties.

Sandra my youngest sister was at home when my mother and father separated. She took advantage of being able to join Betty in America.

Eluned lives in Oxfordshire. She and her husband Ian have now both retired.

Awena lived in Corby all her married life and passed away just before her 50th wedding anniversary. Just before her death, her son Mark moved to North Wales to follow his profession in the N.H.S. and bought a house in Cwm-y-Glo, who would have believed that?

My father never re-married and lived to old age in Corby. My mother married Bert Sayers, a wonderful man who took great care of her for over 25 years of marriage. With all the ups and downs the family remained a family unit and like everything in life we had good and bad times.

All this was not to affect myself as it did my sisters, as I was soon married to Margaret Blakeley and had started a family.   I could write all day about my wonderful wife and my two boys and my grandchildren.   Our marriage has lasted well over 55 years and not only did I gain a good wife, my in-laws were the rock that our marriage was built on.

We have lived in Corby throughout and I have found the town and the people the most helpful working class people you could find. "Help one another" should be the motto for this town. My work took me all over the world and overall I enjoyed my time at work.

With the support of my wife I enjoyed my sports: Cycling, Walking, Bowling, Cricket, you name it and I had a go at it.

My main sport was football playing at a good level, refereeing for 26 years and a member of the F.A. for over 50 years. My proudest moment was being awarded my 50 years award by the F.A, and 40 years membership of the Referees Association. The England .v. Scotland Schoolboys international at Wembley was also special.

Cross country and road running have also been life time sports. From the age of 14 I have been a dedicated runner. The sport has taken me all over the world: Toronto, New York, Malta and Cyprus to name a few. Also being a member of Corby Athletic Club and The Road Runners Club has given me great pleasure.

My aim now is to continue running and enjoy all the things that have given me so much pleasure over the years.

WELSH TERMINOLOGY

Nain	Grandmother
Sid-mai / s'mai	All right?
Ty Capel	Chapel House
Cwt Hers	Hearse Shed
pull heli	Deep water
bara-brith	A Welsh fruit cake – very tasty when well made!
Cwm	Valley
Rhud fach	Lesser ford, or crossing place – a shallow area of the river with gravel underfoot which could be easily splashed across.
Rhud fawr	Greater ford or crossing place
Railway Hotel.	Also known as The Snowdon Inn and Ficsan
Afon Rhythallt.	River Seiont.

Made in the USA
Charleston, SC
09 July 2016